Analogue Guide

New York

Contents

New York

—Welcome to Analogue New York

New York has captured the imagination of would-be New Yorkers across the globe for generations—from those seeking economic opportunity or political freedom, to the beleaguered European aristocrat aiming to reinvent himself, and the American teenager yearning for the vitality of a metropolis. In fact, so many groups have contributed to the making of this great city since its foundation in the 17th century, that it is hard to imagine its reputation as "Capital of the World" changing hands for years to come—and this is before New Yorkers have even been consulted on the matter.

Today's New York is far removed from the grit and grime that the city had become synonymous with by the mid-1980s. A decade of *broken windows* policing and more recent efforts to brand New York as a "luxury product" have turned the city inside out. Its reincarnation is perhaps best captured by the Meatpacking District, where the prostitutes and meat handlers of Adrian Lyne's *Fatal Attraction* have given way to a mix of high-end fashion retail and entertainment.

Sweep aside the gloss and gimmickry, however, and New York unveils the innumerable treasures of its contemporary self—Downtown's excellent coffee outlets, world class theatre and off the beaten track arts, the classy dining establishments of Midtown's power set, and Brooklyn's top-notch locavore fare.

The Analogue Guide provides a short-list of the best of all of this, with photographs and maps throughout. Enjoy!

Neighbourhoods

West Village –p20
With quaint architecture and narrow tree-lined streets, the West Village's identity was forged on the bohemian lifestyle of its residents

SoHo & Tribeca –p8
Celebrated for their 19th century cast iron architecture, SoHo and Tribeca, once neglected, are now prime retail territory

Lower East Side –p44
Traditionally an immigrant neighbourhood, the Lower East Side has since been discovered by those in search of a grittier NYC

Chelsea & Flatiron –p54
Art galleries and media start-ups now abound, making Chelsea and the Flatiron District destinations in and of themselves

NEW JERSEY

NEWARK (15 KM)

CHELSE

WEST VILLAGE

FLA

SOHO

TRIBECA DOWNTOWN

EAST VILLAGE

FINANCIAL DISTRICT

LOWER EAST SIDE

GOVERNORS ISLAND

UPPER BAY

DOWNTOWN

COBBLE HILL

FORT GREENE

BR(

PARK SLOPE PROSPECT HEIGHTS

N

2 kilometres

PROSPECT PARK

JOHN F KENNEDY (15 KM

HUDSON RIVER

UPPER
WEST SIDE   CENTRAL
PARK

HARLEM

UPPER
EAST SIDE

MIDTOWN
N STATION

GRAND CENTRAL

ATTAN   ROOSEVELT
ISLAND

EAST
RIVER

LONG
ISLAND
CITY

QUEENS

LA GUARDIA (2 KM)

BURG

Uptown –p78
The Upper East and West Sides are leafy refuges for the city's movers and shakers. Harlem is on the verge of a second renaissance

Midtown –p64
The city's pulsating commercial and cultural centre—skyscrapers converge here to shape New York's famous skyline

Brooklyn –p92
Once a city in its own right, contemporary Brooklyn is culturally distinct and a hotbed of social and culinary innovation

East Village –p32
At the centre of counterculture since the 1960s, the East Village has morphed into a safer, more popular version of its former self

SoHo & Tribeca
—New York's Cast Iron Heart

SoHo, celebrated for its mid-19th century cast iron architecture and cobbled streets, is in many ways a microcosm of New York's recent history. Once a thriving hub of commercial and social life, the neighbourhood fell into a state of neglect as the city's centre of gravity shifted further uptown. By the mid-20th century, the area had turned into a wasteland of light industry and small manufacturing enterprises. Starting in the 1960s, SoHo's cavernous lofts were discovered by artists seeking inexpensive studio space.

Home to fewer artists today, but still the centre of the city's creative trades, SoHo has since become a much sought-after residential neighbourhood and prime retail destination. Most international fashion and design labels are clustered on and around West Broadway and Prince Street, while the length of Broadway is home to a more predictable retail mix. Cobbled Crosby, Greene and Mercer Streets best demonstrate SoHo's glorious architectural heritage. On a weekday, the area south of Broome Street still feels refreshingly rough around the edges.

While somewhat off the radar only a few years ago, Nolita, SoHo's low-rise extension to the west, has since gained notoriety for the trendiness of its independent boutiques dotting charming Elizabeth, Prince and Mott Streets. To the south, Tribeca shares much of SoHo's architectural heritage and history of decay and revival, and today is a preferred residential address for the suits of nearby Wall Street.

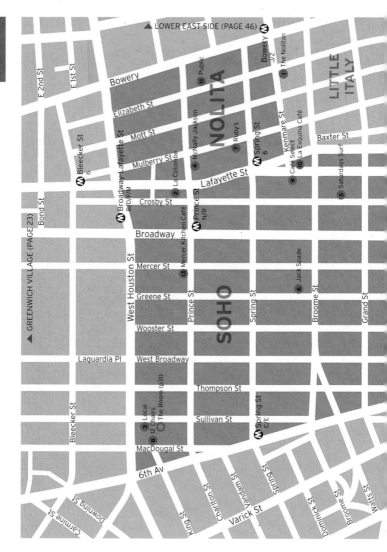

▲ LOWER EAST SIDE (PAGE 46)

◀ GREENWICH VILLAGE (PAGE 23)

NOLITA

LITTLE ITALY

SOHO

Bowery

E 2nd St

E 1st St

Bleecker St

Lafayette St

Elizabeth St

Mott St

Mulberry St

Broadway

Crosby St

Bond St

⑪ Public

Bowery

① The Nolitan

J/Z

④ McNally Jackson

⑦ Ruby's

Spring St
6

Kenmare St

Café Select

⑨ ⑩ La Esquina Café

Baxter St

⑤ Saturdays Surf

② La Colombe

Lafayette St

Ⓜ Prince St
N/R

⑬ Mercer Kitchen Café

Mercer St

Greene St

Prince St

Spring St

⑥ Jack Spade

Broome St

Grand St

West Houston St

Wooster St

Laguardia Pl

West Broadway

Thompson St

Sullivan St

Bleecker St

③ Local

⑧ 12 Chairs   The Room (p31)

MacDougal St

Ⓜ Spring St
C/E

6th Av

Carmine St

Downing St

King St

Charlton St

Vandam St

Spring St

Varick St

Dominick St

Broome St

Watts St

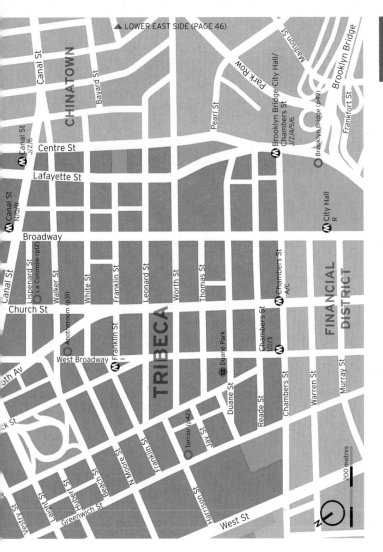

CHINATOWN

Canal St

Bayard St

Canal St
J/Z/6

Centre St

Lafayette St

Canal St
N/Q/R

Broadway

Canal St

Lispenard St

La Colombe (p12)

Walker St

White St

Franklin St

Leonard St

Worth St

Thomas St

Church St

Anotheroom (p31)

Franklin St

West Broadway

TRIBECA

Terroir (p42)

Franklin St

N Moore St

Beach St

Duane St

Reade St

Chambers St

Warren St

Murray St

Jay St

Harrison St

West St

Greenwich St

Hubert St

Laight St

Vestry St

5th Av

ck St

Pearl St

Park Row

Madison St

Brooklyn Bridge

Brooklyn Bridge–City Hall/
Chambers St
J/Z/4/5/6

Brooklyn Bridge (p49)

Frankfort St

City Hall
R

Chambers St
A/C

FINANCIAL
DISTRICT

Chambers St
1/2/3

Duane Park

12

200 metres

N

Nolita Hotel

The Nolitan

🏵 30 Kenmare St, at Elizabeth St
+1 212 925 2555
nolitanhotel.com
Ⓜ Bowery ⓳Ⓩ, Spring St ⑥
Doubles from $227/night incl. tax;
excl. breakfast, available in-house.

A fresh and contemporary
boutique hotel in the heart of
one of Downtown's most alluring
neighbourhoods, The Nolitan
combines casual luxury with
urbane sophistication. Many of the
hotel's fifty-five guestrooms have
private balconies with stunning
views. And for those who have tired
of the neighbourhood's countless
dining options, the hotel's on-site
restaurant Ellabess serves breakfast
and dinner.

Philadelphia Coffee Import

La Colombe

🏵 270 Lafayette St, between West
Houston St and Prince St
+1 212 625 1717
lacolombe.com
Ⓜ Prince St Ⓝ Ⓡ, Broadway-
Lafayette St ⒷⒹⒻⓂ, Spring St ⑥
Open daily. Mon-Fri 7.30am-6.30pm;
Sat/Sun 8.30am-6.30pm.

Philadelphia based roaster La
Colombe serves some of the finest
beans in NYC at its aesthetically
pleasing trio of Manhattan
locations. The cafés boast a
cosmopolitan atmosphere forged
by a strong local following and
international *mélange* of creative
types. Drop by the sun drenched
Nolita location (pictured above)
for a rich and creamy cappuccino
seemingly melting into its Italian
Majolica cup, and a sumptuous
slice of olive oil loaf. Then borrow a
section of the NY Times and relax
on the solid wooden banquette.

Neighbourhood Café

Local

🜺 144 Sullivan St, between West
Houston St and Prince St
+1 212 253 2601
Ⓜ Spring St Ⓒ Ⓔ, Houston St ❶
Open daily. Mon-Fri 7.30am-6pm; Sat
8.30am-6pm; Sun 9am-6pm.

This small, cosy neighbourhood
hangout serves high quality coffee
and a range of sandwiches and
snacks. Local also offers wine and
beer, drawing an after hours crowd
looking to unwind in an unfussy
atmosphere. Exposed brick and
solid wood tables supplement the
café's organic feel. The attractive
public outdoor terrace located
across the sidewalk allows patrons
to bask in the area's architectural
charm.

Books, Magazines and Coffee

McNally Jackson

🜻 52 Prince St, between Lafayette
St and Mulberry St
+1 212 274 1160
mcnallyjackson.com
Ⓜ Prince St Ⓝ Ⓡ, Spring St ❻,
Broadway-Lafayette St Ⓑ Ⓓ Ⓕ Ⓜ
Open daily. Mon-Sat 10am-10pm; Sun
10am-9pm.

In a neighbourhood that has
seen rapid gentrification, McNally
Jackson offers an oasis of
intellectual respite. Characterized
by its convivial atmosphere and
soothing decor, the store is at the
forefront of international literary
trends. Its team hand selects an
inspiring collection of magazines,
new and classical international
fiction (also in Spanish and French)
and non-fiction to be devoured,
along with pastries, at the
shop's café. Readings by premier
international authors are scheduled
regularly.

Surf Shop & Coffee Counter

Saturdays Surf

⑤ 31 Crosby St, between Broome St and Grand St

+1 212 966 7875

saturdaysnyc.com

Ⓜ Spring St ⑥, Canal St Ⓝ Ⓠ Ⓡ, Canal St Ⓙ Ⓩ ⑥

Open daily. Mon-Fri 8.30am-7pm; Sat/Sun 10am-7pm.

Saturdays Surf presents a unique concept with a distinctly Pacific vibe. The shabby-chic store offers a vast array of surfing paraphernalia including boards, wetsuits, books and artwork dedicated to the wave—while doubling as an excellent café serving La Colombe blends. Grab a flat white and browse the selection of books dedicated to Australian, Californian and South African tides. Then head back to the gloriously dishevelled garden courtyard to finish off your cup in the afternoon sun.

Home of the Messenger Bag

Jack Spade

⑥ 56 Greene St, between Spring St and Broome St

+1 212 625 1820

jackspade.com

Ⓜ Prince St Ⓝ Ⓡ, Spring St ⑥

Open daily. Mon-Sat 11am-7pm; Sun noon-6pm.

Located on a gorgeous cobblestone block at the centre of SoHo's Cast Iron District, the original Jack Spade store continues to deliver the brand's high quality functionality-meets-design range of messenger bags. Crafted out of waxed cotton and heavy canvas, the bags were first sold to industrial clients before re-inventing themselves as beautifully sturdy minimalist work horses for the chic and intellectual. The store itself is peppered with authentic vintage paraphernalia, reminiscent of SoHo's recent history as a creative workshop.

Aussie-Style Burgers
Ruby's

219 Mulberry St, between Prince St and Spring St
+1 212 925 5755
rubyscafe.us
Ⓜ Spring St Ⓖ, Prince St Ⓝ Ⓡ
Open daily 10am-10.30pm. Summer: 9am-10.30pm.

Perfectly executed Aussie-style burgers, named after Sydney's numerous beaches, burst with flavor at this tiny Nolita institution. Expats rub shoulders with the local fashion crowd at the buzzing communal tables, while Nolita-meets-Little Italy shoppers thronging Mulberry Street percolate into the space. Enjoy the relaxed vibe by kicking back with a Bronte and pretending you're on Bondi.

Eastern Mediterranean Hospitality
12 Chairs

Ⓑ 56 MacDougal St, between West Houston St and Prince St
+1 212 254 8640
Ⓜ Spring St Ⓒ Ⓔ, Houston St Ⓐ
Open daily. Sun-Thu 8am-11pm; Fri/Sat 8am-midnight.

This wonderfully unpretentious Israeli café/restaurant on the pretty western side of SoHo is an excellent brunch and casual dinner spot. Photography of Israeli urban life adorns the walls and a fusion of Israeli and American dishes is served round the clock. The hummus and warm pita bread is divine. After the meal, stroll around the neighbourhood to take in the array of fire escapes drizzling the facades of the surrounding tenement buildings.

Solid Swiss Fare

Café Select

9 212 Lafayette St, at Kenmare St
+1 212 925 9322
cafeselectnyc.com
M Spring St **6**, Prince St **N R**
Open daily from 9am-late.

This Swiss brasserie offers a range
of Alpine classics served in a
modernist setting, while a giant
Rolex clock infuses the scene with
Bahnhofstrasse glamour. A meal at
Select could consist of *Bratwurst*
with *Rösti*, muesli pancakes, *tête de
moine* raw cow's cheese and a glass
of Swiss chasselas, all served with
characteristic panache. The zinc bar
is a great spot to grab a pre or post-
SoHo *Schale* (café latte) or beer.

Chic Mexican Cantina

La Esquina Café

10 114 Kenmare St, at Lafayette St
(entrance on Lafayette St)
+1 646 613 7100
esquinanyc.com
M Spring St **6**, Prince St **N R**
Open daily. Dinner Sun-Thu 5pm-
midnight; Sat/Sun 5pm-1am. Lunch
Mon-Fri noon-4pm. Brunch Sat/Sun
11am-3.45pm.

La Esquina Café is the laid back,
elegant "middle child" of the
Esquina triumvirate of Mexican
restaurants. Serving three meals a
day, the space can be dressed up
or down depending on the time
of day, and is an excellent place
to grab some fresh fish tacos and
other solid Mexican dishes. The
recessed bookshelves and tasteful
Mexican posters add a touch of
class, while the string of local
hipsters sipping Negra Modelos
remind you that this is indeed
Nolita.

Michelin-Starred Nolita Dining

Public

Burlesque Southern Comfort

Duane Park

⑪ 210 Elizabeth St, between Prince St and Spring St
+1 212 343 7011
public-nyc.com
Ⓜ Bowery ❶❷, 2 Av ❻, Spring St ❻
Open daily. Dinner Mon-Thu 6pm-11pm; Fri/Sat 6pm-midnight; Sun 6pm-10.30pm. Brunch Sat/Sun 11am-3.30pm.

This Michelin star winning Australian restaurant tops several criteria for casual excellence. Flanked by Elizabeth Street's custom furniture design shops and sheltered from the area's cacophonous patches, Public brings a sense of elegance to Nolita. Dishes are characterized by an unmistakable antipodean bent—New Zealand venison loin makes an appearance, as does Barossa Shiraz. The industrial sized space is divided into several annexes, underscored by raw exposed brick and light Pacific-style furniture.

⑫ 157 Duane St, between Hudson St and West Broadway
+1 212 732 5555
duaneparknyc.com
Ⓜ Chambers St ❶❷❸, Chambers St ❹❻
Closed Sun/Mon. Dinner Tue-Thu 5.30pm-11pm; Fri/Sat 6pm-midnight. Lunch Tue-Fri noon-3pm.

Reflecting the provenance of its owners, Duane Park represents a felicitous mix of Southern elegance and British restraint—sumptuously decorated with plush blue velvet chairs, reclaimed chandeliers from Louisiana and oversized antique mirrors. The menu features succulent creole classics with a twist. Renowned burlesque nights are organized to accompany dinner on Fridays and Saturdays. Duane Park offers a whimsical, tasteful addition to the typically more conventional, corporate Tribeca dining scene.

SoHo Shopping Break

Mercer Kitchen Café

🔵13 99 Prince St, at Mercer St
+1 212 966 5454
mercerhotel.com
Ⓜ Prince St Ⓝ Ⓡ, Broadway-
Lafayette St Ⓑ Ⓓ Ⓕ Ⓜ
Open daily. Mon-Thu 7am-1am; Fri/
Sat 7am-2am; Sun 7am-midnight.

Sandwiched between the adjacent
guests-only lounge and the dining
scene downstairs, the Mercer
Kitchen's upstairs café provides an
intimate spot designed for a quiet
tête-a-tête over a pot of afternoon
tea or an evening cocktail. Located
in the very heart of SoHo, the
brasserie/bar serves as a pampering
ground in which to recover from
the ravages of a hard afternoon of
shopping—or simply to relish in the
singular pleasure of an after dinner
nightcap.

The West Village

—Perfect Urban Village Life

The West Village, with its panoply of narrow streets and quaint architecture, was reputed for the bohemian lifestyle of its residents long before other Manhattan neighbourhoods became fashionable. As early as in the late 19th century, the area was known for its artistic denizens and as a centre of alternative culture and progressive thought. As a rural hamlet dating from the 17th century, the West Village had a thriving population when the city's street grid was drawn up over Manhattan farmland two centuries later. Already built-up, the neighbourhood fortuitously retained its intricate "off the grid" web of one-way streets, to the consistent bafflement and occasional chagrin of NYC cab drivers.

Today, despite proving equally alluring to bankers and movie stars as to bohemian types, the West Village has preserved its unique flavor. The neighbourhood boasts stunning tree-lined residential streets, amongst which Perry and Charles Streets are notable, and is populated by an impressive array of small cafés. The neighbourhood also remains a nexus of downtown nightlife, especially along gentrified Hudson Street and slightly seedy Christopher Street. Bleecker Street is known for its fashion outlets and the occasional cupcake boutique.

Beyond Hudson Street, the Far West Village offers a more low key experience, hosting some excellent cafés and intimate but casual bars. Further north, the Meatpacking District can feel overdeveloped in its retail and nightlife frenzy.

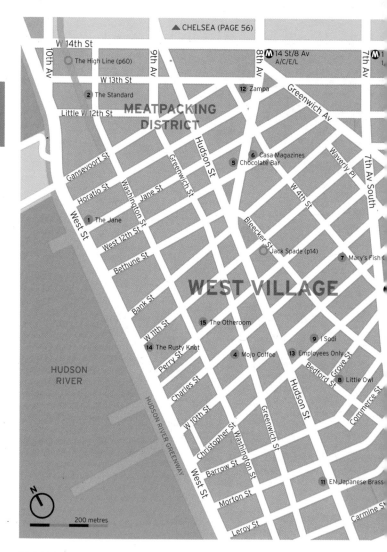

W 14th St

10th Av

9th Av

○ The High Line (p60)

8th Av

Ⓜ 14 St/8 Av
A/C/E/L

7th Av

Ⓜ 1
1

W 13th St

2 The Standard

12 Zampa

Greenwich Av

Little W 12th St

MEATPACKING DISTRICT

Hudson St

6 Casa Magazines
5 Chocolate Bar

Waverly Pl

7th Av South

Gansevoort St

Greenwich St

W 4th St

Horatio St

Jane St

Washington St

West St

1 The Jane

West 12th St

Bleecker St

○ Jack Spade (p14)

7 Mary's Fish C

Bethune St

Bank St

WEST VILLAGE

W 11th St

15 The Otheroom

14 The Rusty Knot

4 Mojo Coffee

9 I Sodi

13 Employees Only

Grove St

Perry St

Bedford St

8 Little Owl

HUDSON RIVER

Charles St

Commerce St

Hudson St

W 10th St

Christopher St

Washington St

Greenwich St

HUDSON RIVER GREENWAY

Barrow St

11 EN Japanese Brass

West St

Morton St

Carmine St

Leroy St

N

200 metres

PAGE 22   THE WEST VILLAGE

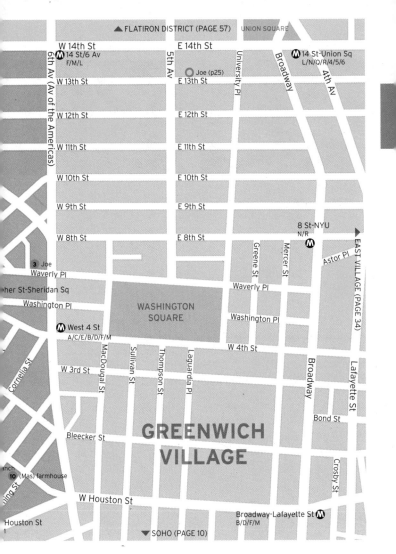

▲ FLATIRON DISTRICT (PAGE 57) UNION SQUARE

W 14th St
E 14th St

Ⓜ 14 St/6 Av
F/M/L

Ⓜ 14 St-Union Sq
L/N/Q/R/4/5/6

Ⓞ Joe (p25)

W 13th St
E 13th St

W 12th St
E 12th St

W 11th St
E 11th St

W 10th St
E 10th St

W 9th St
E 9th St

W 8th St
E 8th St

8 St-NYU
N/R Ⓜ

3 Joe

Waverly Pl

Waverly Pl

...her St-Sheridan Sq

Washington Pl

Washington Pl

WASHINGTON
SQUARE

Ⓜ West 4 St
A/C/E/B/D/F/M

W 4th St

W 3rd St

Bleecker St

GREENWICH
VILLAGE

10 ...(Mas) farmhouse

W Houston St

Broadway-Lafayette St Ⓜ
B/D/F/M

Houston St

▼ SOHO (PAGE 10)

6th Av (Av of the Americas)

5th Av

University Pl

Broadway

4th Av

Greene St

Mercer St

Astor Pl

EAST VILLAGE (PAGE 34)

Cornelia St

MacDougal St

Sullivan St

Thompson St

Laguardia Pl

Broadway

Lafayette St

Bond St

Crosby St

Hotel on the Hudson

The Jane

① 113 Jane St, at West St
+1 212 924 6700
thejanenyc.com
Ⓜ 14 St/8 Av Ⓐ Ⓒ Ⓔ Ⓛ
Doubles from $262/night incl.
tax; bunkbed cabin (communal
bathroom) from $117/night incl. tax;
excl. breakfast, available in-house.

The Jane offers a civilized choice
of lodging in a handsome setting.
The hotel's location in the relative
seclusion of the Far West Village
belies its ready accessibility to the
rest of Manhattan. In the early 20th
century, The Jane was a regular
haunt of sailors. These days, an in-
house branch of Nolita's Café Gitane
complements the venue's overall
boho flair, while the hotel bar is
sumptuously tattered.

Spectacular Views

The Standard

② 848 Washington St, at West
13th St
+1 212 645 4646
standardhotels.com
Ⓜ 14 St/8 Av Ⓐ Ⓒ Ⓔ Ⓛ
Doubles from $445/night incl. tax;
excl. breakfast, available in-house.

Serial hotelier Andre Balazs' West
Side venture is a retro-futuristic
glass and steel structure towering
over the High Line Park (p60) and
the abattoir-turned-boutique
warehouses of the Meatpacking
District. With unabashed flair, this
Hudson-meets-the-Jetsons affair
offers all the conveniences of a
luxury hotel in a playful setting. The
Top of the Standard bar provides
the *mise en scène* for jaw dropping
panoramic Manhattan views,
intriguingly best beheld from the
bar's dramatic restrooms. Reserve a
table in advance to fully indulge in
the view.

Manhattan Coffee Authority

Joe

3 141 Waverly Place, between Christopher St and 6th Av
+1 212 924 6750
joetheartofcoffee.com
M West 4 St **A C E B D F M**, Christopher St-Sheridan Sq **1**
Open daily. Mon-Fri 7am-8pm; Sat/Sun 8am-8pm.

A sun-drenched café with a light and festive air on a typical West Village block, Joe on Waverly Place is the original of eight locations of this contemporary NYC classic. The espresso-based beverages are consistently excellent, and the unusually high quality of the soy-based drinks deserves particular mention. In addition to fulfilling its café functions, Joe offers a series of classes, centred on the art of the seductive bean.

Relaxed Café in the Far West

Mojo Coffee

4 128 Charles St, at Greenwich St
+1 212 691 6656
mojo-nyc.com
M Christopher St-Sheridan Sq **1**, West 4 St **A C E B D F M**
Open daily. Mon-Fri 6.30am-8pm; Sat/Sun 7.30am-8pm.

Exposed brick, leafy plants and caramel wood panelling set the tone for Mojo's wholly organic selection of coffees, locally sourced dairy products, soups, salads and sandwiches. A fabulous place to relax with the weekend edition of the New York Times—perhaps after an invigorating run along the Hudson River Greenway, located just a few blocks down the street.

Chocolate Boutique & Café

Chocolate Bar

⑤ 19 8th Av, between Jane St and West 12th St

+1 212 366 1541

chocolatebarnyc.com

Ⓜ 14 St/8 Av Ⓐ Ⓒ Ⓔ Ⓛ, 14 St ① ② ③

Open daily. Mon-Sat 7.30am-10pm; Sun 8am-9pm.

Resplendent as a small jewel, bijou sized Chocolate Bar specializes in all things cacao, while also serving excellent coffee and tea. Its signature line of chocolates are hand poured in the city, and their wrappings custom designed by local artists. The space has a smooth, sophisticated feel, reflected in the appropriately brown tonality of its interior decoration.

Everything That's Fit to Print

Casa Magazines

⑥ 22 8th Av, between Jane St and West 12 St

+1 212 645 1197

Ⓜ 14 St/8 Av Ⓐ Ⓒ Ⓔ Ⓛ, 14 St ① ② ③

Open daily 6am-midnight.

This small corner shop offers one of New York's most comprehensive selections of international newspapers and magazines. Whether you're looking for a paper copy of *Le Monde* to go with your morning coffee, or a specialist publication about the Milan fashion scene, Casa Magazines stocks it— and if they don't, they will be happy to order it for you.

Tantalizing Fish Restaurant

Mary's Fish Camp

7 64 Charles St, at West 4th St
+1 646 486 2185
marysfishcamp.com
Ⓜ Christopher St-Sheridan Sq **1**,
West 4 St **Ⓐ Ⓒ Ⓔ Ⓑ Ⓓ Ⓕ Ⓜ**
Closed Sun. Lunch noon-3pm.
Dinner 6pm-11pm.

A casually chic affair taking fish to new heights, Mary's Fish Camp is equally alluring for both lunch and dinner. With unwavering respect for seasonal and local produce, this fish camp serves up a branzino like no other. Large windows and a convivial fish bar make for a lively atmosphere both inside the restaurant and along its flanks. The surrounding streets are some of the West Village's most picturesque.

Romantic Corner Restaurant

Little Owl

8 90 Bedford St, at Grove St
+1 212 741 4695
thelittleowlnyc.com
Ⓜ Christopher St-Sheridan Sq **1**,
West 4 St **Ⓐ Ⓒ Ⓔ Ⓑ Ⓓ Ⓕ Ⓜ**
Open daily. Dinner Mon-Sat 5pm-11pm; Sun 5pm-10pm. Lunch Mon-Fri noon-2.30pm. Brunch Sat/Sun 10.30am-2.30pm.

A small classic located on a characteristically romantic corner of the leafy West Village, Little Owl performs a modern twist on classical dishes while respecting seasonal dynamics. The results are staggeringly delicious. It is advisable to book well in advance to secure a table. That said, as a date night favourite, a few tables for two are available for walk-ins.

Tuscan Restaurant

I Sodi

9 105 Christopher St, between Hudson St and Bleecker St
+1 212 414 5774
isodinyc.com
M Christopher St-Sheridan Sq **1**, West 4 St **A** **C** **E** **B** **D** **F** **M**
Open daily. Dinner: 5.30pm-10pm or later. Brunch Sat/Sun noon-3.30pm.

This intricate restaurant offers delicious hand crafted pasta and tantalizing *secondi* in a refined setting—a wonderful addition to the diverse trappings of Christopher Street. A terrific selection of Italian wines can be ordered by the quartino, allowing for a greater degree of oenological flexibility as the evening progresses. Pasta dishes are available in half portions to go along with the changes of quartino.

Southern French Fine Dining

Mas (farmhouse)

10 39 Downing St, between 7th Av South and Bedford St
+1 212 255 1790
masfarmhouse.com
M Houston St **1**, West 4 St **A** **C** **E** **B** **D** **F** **M**
Open daily 6pm-11.30pm.

An excellent restaurant for serious foodies who prefer a more laid back downtown vibe to the formal strictures of the Uptown culinary scene. Southern French cuisine, influenced by local seasonal produce, is meticulously prepared. Intellectual ingredient combinations create bursts of intense flavor that reverberate on the palate for minutes and are thoughtfully accentuated by the excellent wine selection. As the name suggests, the decor is reminiscent of a contemporary farmhouse.

Japanese with Flair

EN  Japanese Brasserie

⑪ 435 Hudson St, between Morton St and Leroy St

+1 212 647 9196

enjb.com

Ⓜ Houston St ❶, West 4 St ⒶⒸⒺ ⒷⒹⒻⓂ

Open daily. Dinner Sun-Thu 5.30pm-10.30pm; Fri/Sat 5.30pm-11.30pm. Lunch Mon-Fri noon-2.30pm. Brunch Sat/Sun 11am-2.30pm.

EN is the dramatically elegant New York City incarnation of a Japanese group of restaurants. A staggering selection of sake and shochu meld with an array of beautifully prepared Japanese small plates. The tofu is handmade, delicate and divine and the *gindara*, or black cod, simply melts in your mouth. All of the gorgeous interior decoration was imported from Japan. The restaurant's proximity to the bars of the West Village makes it a great launch pad for a night out.

Italian Wine Bar and Kitchen

Zampa

⑫ 306 West 13th St, between West 4th St and 8th Av

+1 212 206 0601

zampanyc.com

Ⓜ 14 St/8 Av ⒶⒸⒺⓁ, 14 St ❶❷❸

Open daily. Mon-Fri 8am-midnight; Sat 11am-midnight; Sun 11am-4pm (brunch) and 5pm-10pm (dinner).

Located at the junction of the West Village and the Meatpacking District, Zampa is a true double-neighbourhood gem. The restaurant specializes in Italian wines and small plates, but also prepares excellent full sized dinner dishes. The bar and front of the restaurant buzz with energy as the evening progresses—reserving a table in the back allows you to soak in the atmosphere without becoming engulfed by it.

Hudson Street Hideaway

Employees Only

⑬ 510 Hudson St, between West 10th St and Christopher St
+1 212 242 3021
employeesonlynyc.com
Ⓜ Christopher St-Sheridan Sq **①**, West 4 St **ⒶⒸⒺⒷⒹⒻⓂ**
Open daily. Dinner 6pm-midnight. Late night dinner midnight-3.30am.

This speakeasy and restaurant is an unusual affair. Popular with members of the city's food and beverage industries during their off hours, "EO" specializes in artisanal cocktails crafted with traditional ingredients. The bar takes on something of a burlesque feel toward the early hours and the restaurant is perpetually abuzz with chatter of both business and pleasure, reflecting a stalwart NYC heritage.

Maritime Bar

The Rusty Knot

⑭ 425 West St, at West 11th St
+1 212 645 5668
therustyknot.com
Ⓜ Christopher St-Sheridan Sq **①**, West 4 St **ⒶⒸⒺⒷⒹⒻⓂ**
Open daily. Sun-Fri from 5.30pm-late; Sat from 2pm-late.

On the far fringes of the West Village, practically in the Hudson River, lies a wonderful watering hole known as the Rusty Knot. The funky brainchild of Ken Friedman (of the nearby Spotted Pig) and Taavo Somer (of Freeman's, p50), the bar serves up a selection of beers, cocktails and wines in a whimsical maritime setting.

Neighbourhood Hangout
The Otheroom

⑮ 143 Perry St, between Washington St and Greenwich St
+1 212 645 9758
theotheroom.com
Ⓜ Christopher St-Sheridan Sq ❶, West 4 St ⒶⒸⒺⒷⒹⒻⓂ
Open daily. Sun/Mon 5pm-2am; Tue-Sat 5pm-4am.

The Otheroom is a seductive, dimly lit beer and wine bar in the Far West Village. One of the neighbourhood's more extensive wine lists is on offer, with over sixty intriguing bottles to choose from. On warmer days, the front windows are flung open, allowing the picturesque Village streetscape to waft into the bar's candle lit interior. The bar's siblings, the Room in SoHo and Anotheroom in Tribeca, are equally inviting.

Speakeasy
Little Branch

⑯ 20 7th Av South, at Leroy St
+1 212 929 4360
littlebranch.net
Ⓜ Houston St ❶, West 4 St ⒶⒸⒺ ⒷⒹⒻⓂ
Open daily 7pm-3am.

In typical speakeasy fashion, this hidden cocktail den crafts intoxicating classics in a narrow L-shaped lounge located in an underground lair far beneath the reaches of 7th Avenue South. The crowd falls somewhere between intellectual and hipster, uniformly indulging in top class Martinis served at semi-hidden booths scattered throughout this secretive temple of mixology.

The East Village
—Counterculture Meets Commerce

The East Village was historically part of the Lower East Side (p44) but developed a distinct identity when hippies, musicians and artists moved into the area in the 1960s. St Marks Place, once the epicentre of the East Village's counterculture, has retained much of its grungy character and nightlife, today doubling as a playground for students from nearby New York University. The area is also home to a significant Japanese expat scene, catered to by a host of sushi, sake and karaoke bars.

As the East Village became a safer place in the 1990s, it experienced an influx of new, more mainstream residents. Today, the streets between Broadway and 1st Avenue are lined with small shops, restaurants and cafés catering to an increasingly urbane clientele. East 9th Street in particular boasts a wide array of small boutiques and other independent retail. Between Broadway and the Bowery, NoHo's cobbled streets, closer in feel to SoHo than to the East Village, have gained a reputation for sophistication and fabulously pricey loft real estate.

On the far side of Tompkins Square Park, Alphabet City, named after its lettered avenues, has retained more of the neighbourhood's countercultural edge and immigrant character. The area plays host to a large share of the neighbourhood's innovative and quirky small businesses.

UNION SQUARE

E 14th St

14 St-Union Sq
L/N/Q/R/4/5/6

3rd Av

3 Av
L

2nd Av

1st Av

E 13th St

E 12th St

12 Pata Ne

E 11th St

E 10th St

3 Stogo

Broadway

4th Av

E 9th St

Stuyvesant St

11 Hasaki

4 Sakaya

GREENWICH VILLAGE (PAGE 23)

E 8th St

8 St-NYU
N/R

Astor Pl

Astor Pl
6

St Marks Pl

Greene St

Mercer St

Astor Pl

Lafayette St

Cooper Sq

E 7th St

1 Abraço

Waverly Pl

E 6th St

Washington Pl

La Colombe (p12)

E 5th St

8 Jewel Bak

W 4th St

E 4th St

E 4th St

W 3rd St

Great Jones St

Bowery

E 3rd St

NOHO

Bond St

E 2nd St

10 Il Buco

Bleecker St

6 Prune **2** Bluebi

Bleecker St
6

Crosby St

Mulberry St

Mott St

Elizabeth St

E 1st St

5 Liz Christy Garden

E Houston St

2 Av
F

Forsyth St

Eldridge St

Allen St

N

200 metres

Broadway-Lafayette St
B/D/F/M

▼ NOLITA (PAGE 10)

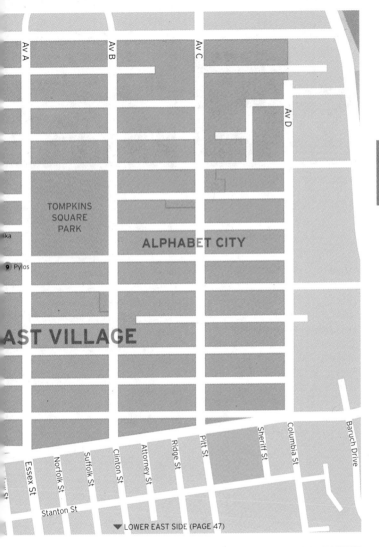

Av A

Av B

Av C

Av D

ika

9 Pylos

TOMPKINS
SQUARE
PARK

ALPHABET CITY

AST VILLAGE

Essex St

Norfolk St

Suffolk St

Clinton St

Attorney St

Ridge St

Pitt St

Sheriff St

Columbia St

Baruch Drive

Stanton St

▼ LOWER EAST SIDE (PAGE 47)

Espresso & Semi-Sweets

Abraço

1 86 East 7th St, between 1st Av and 2nd Av
abraconyc.com
Ⓜ 2 Av **Ⓕ**, Astor Pl **6**
Closed Mon. Open Tue-Sat 8am-4pm. Sun 9am-4pm.

Fabulously intense coffee is delightfully accompanied by moist sections of olive oil pound cake, thick slices of *pain perdu* and a host of other seasonal delights at this tiny East Village café with a 70s Brazilian twist. Abraço is an absolute joy for a quick cup on the run or an invigorating after lunch pick-me-up. The premium quality of the espresso at this establishment is guaranteed to animate even the weariest traveller.

Café on First Street

Bluebird Coffee Shop

2 72 East 1st St, at 1st Av
+1 212 260 1879
bluebirdcoffeeshop.com
Ⓜ 2 Av **Ⓕ**, Bleecker St **6**
Open daily. Mon-Sat 8am-7pm; Sun 9am-7pm.

Bluebird is a delightful boutique coffee shop serving excellent espresso drinks. Windows are opened in the summer, allowing customers to sit on high stools lining both the inside and outside of the café. In the winter, the cosy nautical blue and nutty dark wood decor makes this a spot of choice for a cup of high quality brew. East 1st Street is an interesting block to explore as it bridges the atmosphere between the edgy East Village to the north and postcard pretty Nolita to the south.

Non-Dairy Ice Cream

Stogo

③ 159 2nd Av, at East 10th St
(entrance on East 10th St)
+1 212 677 2301
stogonyc.com
Ⓜ Astor Pl Ⓖ, 8 St-NYU Ⓝ Ⓡ, 3 Av Ⓛ
Open daily. Sun-Thu noon-11pm; Fri/
Sat noon-midnight. Winter: opens
30mins later and closes 30mins
earlier.

Stogo specializes in luxuriously
dense organic non-dairy ice cream
across a spectrum of flavours,
served in biodegradable cups.
Ideal for those sweltering New
York summer days or the perfect
complement to a rich espresso
in the form of an *affogato*. Stogo
works with local establishments
such as Fine and Raw Chocolates
and vegan Lower East Side bakery
Babycakes to provide healthy
delights to accompany their
artisanally crafted ice creams.

Purveyor of Fine Sake

Sakaya

④ 324 East 9th St, between 1st Av
and 2nd Av
+1 212 505 7253
sakayanyc.com
Ⓜ Astor Pl Ⓖ, 8 St-NYU Ⓝ Ⓡ, 3 Av Ⓛ
Open daily. Mon-Sat noon-8pm. Sun
noon-7pm.

Ensconced in a gorgeous East
9th Street block, Sakaya stocks a
tremendous and fascinating range
of sake, shochu and other Japanese
spirits. The owners, Rick and Hiroko
frequently travel to new breweries,
unearthing the rare and exquisite
gems that line the shop's walls.
The store is subtly decorated with
warm wooden shelves bathed
in soft light, exuding a sense of
earthy wellbeing. The numerous
bottles, arranged according to their
category and style, are as much a
feast for the eyes as for the palate.

Urban Jungle

Community Gardens

🔵5 East Houston St, between 2nd Av and Bowery

evpcnyc.org

Ⓜ 2 Av 🟠F, Bleecker St 🟢6

Most gardens are open to the public on weekends. Liz Christy Garden: Sat noon-4pm; May-Sep also: Sun noon-4pm; Tue/Thu 6pm-dusk.

Lack of green space and the urban decay of recession-torn 1970s New York prompted a group of East Villagers, led by Liz Christy, to turn vacant lots into small community gardens. Many of the gardens have maintained their radical nature to this day, despite the efforts of the city's omnipotent real estate lobby. The delightful Liz Christy Community Garden, the first of its kind, is easily accessible—located at the corner of Houston Street and the Bowery.

French-Style Brunch

Prune

🟢6 54 East 1st St, between 1st Av and 2nd Av

+1 212 677 6221

prunerestaurant.com

Ⓜ 2 Av 🟠F, Bleecker St 🟢6

Open daily. Dinner 5.30pm-11pm. Lunch Mon-Fri 11.30am-3.30pm. Brunch Sat/Sun 10am-3.30pm.

Prune's festive ambiance melds excellent French inspired country cooking with celebratory spark. The quail is mouth-wateringly tender and the wine list is extensive and unconventional. Though the East 1st Street location and vibe are unmistakably downtown, serious Uptown foodies travel lengths to dine here. Brunch or dinner at Prune can be combined with a stroll in the East Village, SoHo or Nolita, as the location is at the nexus of several exciting neighbourhoods.

Alpine Italian Dining

Paprika

7 110 St Marks Place, between Av A and 1st Av

+1 212 677 6563

paprikarestaurant.com

M 1 Av **L**, 2 Av **F**, Astor Pl **6**

Open daily. Dinner: Mon-Thu 5pm-11pm; Fri/Sat 5pm-11.30pm; Sun 5pm-10.30pm. Brunch 11am-4pm.

On a snowy winter's evening, Paprika brings a touch of the Italian Alps to St Mark's Place. Dishes are simple and rustic, but explode with flavor. The mostly Italian wine list pairs perfectly with entrees such as *pappardelle* with braised oxtail ragu and tender handmade *gnocchi*. Salads are fresh and crisp. Paprika delivers a convivial, unpretentious experience for every season.

Modern Japanese Classic

Jewel Bako

8 239 East 5th St, between 2nd Av and 3rd Av

+1 212 979 1012

M Astor Pl **6**, 2 Av **F**

Closed Sun. Open Mon-Sat 6.30pm-11pm.

We're unsure whether its name, which means "Jewel Box", alludes to the restaurant's bijou design or the collection of small culinary treasures housed in its belly. Either way, this is a cracking little venue. From the soft natural green banquette to the gently curving wooden ceiling, Jewel Bako's casual elegance contrasts with the East Village's rough around the edges ambience. The sushi and sashimi dishes are fresh, innovative and delicious.

Excellent Greek

Pylos

9 128 East 7th St, between Av A and 1st Av

+1 212 473 0220

pylosrestaurant.com

M 2 Av **F**, 1 Av **L**, Astor Pl **6**

Open daily. Dinner Sun-Thu 5pm-midnight; Fri/Sat 5pm-1am. Lunch/Brunch Wed-Sun 11.30am-4pm.

A lamb shank from heaven, mezze from paradise. Tucked in a rough-and-tumble corner of the East Village, Pylos offers unpretentious comfort in an inviting setting. The ceiling above the dining room is precariously lined with row upon row of earthenware, adding to an evening's excitement. Sample wine from the Greek varietals *Assyrtiko* (white) or *Agiorgitiko* (red) with your dish and revel in the hubbub of the crowd.

Rustic Italian

Il Buco

10 47 Bond St, between Lafayette St and Bowery

+1 212 533 1932

ilbuco.com

M Bleecker St **6**, Broadway-Lafayette St **B D F M**

Open daily. Dinner Mon-Thu 6pm-11pm; Fri/Sat 6pm-midnight; Sun 5pm-10.30pm. Lunch Mon-Sat noon-4pm.

Il Buco uses only the freshest organic ingredients sourced from local greenmarkets—complemented by Italian imports for hard to find components. The cellar-like dining room is candlelit, and wine barriques abound. Should you delve into the depths of the underground floor (reserved for private parties), you will discover a secret wine *cave* replete with oenological treasures.

East Village Classic

Hasaki

⑪ 210 East 9th St, at Stuyvesant Street
+1 212 473 3327
hasakinyc.com
Ⓜ Astor Pl ⑥, 8 St-NYU Ⓝ Ⓡ
Open daily. Dinner Sun-Thu 5.30pm-11pm; Fri/Sat 5.30pm-11.30pm. Lunch Wed-Fri noon-3pm; Sat/Sun 1pm-4pm.

Hasaki is a mellow Japanese classic specializing in ridiculously fresh sushi. East 9th Street houses a host of Japanese restaurants, among which Hasaki consistently proves the most refined. Dinner is equally enjoyable at the sushi counter and in the dining area, depending on your preferred level of interaction with the sushi chef. Specials are updated nightly and a there is a no reservations policy.

Spanish Sophisticate

Pata Negra

⑫ 345 East 12th St, between 1st Av and 2nd Av
+1 212 228 1696
patanegratapas.com
Ⓜ 1 Av Ⓛ, Astor Pl ⑥
Open daily. Sun-Tue 5pm-midnight; Wed/Thu 5pm-1am; Fri/Sat 5pm-2am.

Pata Negra is an authentic and sophisticated contemporary Spanish wine and tapas bar tucked in a vibrant corner of the East Village. Sit at one of the elegant high tables and sample the extensive selection of *jamón*, including the eponymous *pata negra*. Other dazzling selections include *pulpo a la gallega*, *wagyu* beef meatballs and a vast selection of Spanish cheeses—or stick to a glass of Rioja and some delicious marcona almonds and spiced olives.

Riesling HQ

Terroir

13 413 East 12th St, between Av A
and 1st Av
+1 646 602 1300
restauranthearth.com
M 1 Av **L**, Astor Pl **6**
Open daily. Mon-Sat 5pm-2am. Sun
5pm-midnight.

Terroir is an excellent, if somewhat
esoteric wine bar. Co-owner Paul
Grieco is a huge fan of the vinously
underappreciated, so expect an
extensive selection of rieslings,
sherries and other such delights.
Mini "taste" portions allow guests to
expand their oenological repertoire
while enjoying a smattering of
small plates. Seating is available at
the communal table or along the
bar. Drop by during the summer
riesling festivities for an in-depth
tête-à-tête with the racy Germano-
Alsacien *cépage*.

The Lower East Side

—Manhattan's Final Frontier

An ethnically diverse immigrant neighbourhood throughout most of its existence, the Lower East side is, in many respects, Manhattan's final frontier. The neighbourhood plays a particular role as a centre of Jewish culture in America and is still home to a vibrant orthodox community. More recently, the area saw an influx of Latin American immigrants followed by a bohemian crowd in search of the urban grit lost in most other parts of contemporary New York.

Orchard Street south of Delancey and the area around Stanton Street are filled with cafés, restaurants and independent boutiques. Further south, beyond Grand Street, the Lower East Side takes on a more low key feel and a distinctly Chinese character as tourists give way to galleries, and the neighborhood merges fairly seamlessly into adjacent Chinatown.

Chinatown developed in the second half of the 19th century in what was then an urban slum around Bayard and Pell Streets. In the decades after America's progressive 1960s immigration reforms, new residents helped Chinatown push its boundaries into the Lower East Side and north across Canal Street into what remains of Little Italy today. Still thoroughly Chinese, the area's fresh (and cheap) produce and central location have more recently been discovered by those venturing beyond the well-trodden paths of other Downtown neighbourhoods.

▲ EAST VILLAGE (PAGE 34)

East H

M Broadway-Lafayette St
B/D/F/M

Broadway

Crosby St

Lafayette St

Mulberry St

Mott St

Elizabeth St

Bowery

Prince St

M 2 Av
F

Chrystie St

Forsyth St

9 Sunshine Cinema

Allen St

Orchard St

Stanton

6 Freemans

7 Rayuela

NOLITA

Rivingto

M Spring St
6

Spring St

Kenmare St

M Bowery
J/Z

SARA D ROOSEVELT PARK

Delance

Broome St

Baxter St

Centre St

Lafayette St

8 Sorella

Broome

10

Grand St

M Grand St
B/D

Grand St

◄ SOHO & TRIBECA (PAGE 10)

Howard St

LITTLE ITALY

Hester St

Hester St

5

Canal St

M Canal St
J/Z/6

Walker St

White St

Canal St

CHINATOWN

3 Eldridge St Synago

Bayard St

4 Forsyth St

Manhattan Bridge

Pike St

East

Pell St

Division St

Market St

N

200 metres

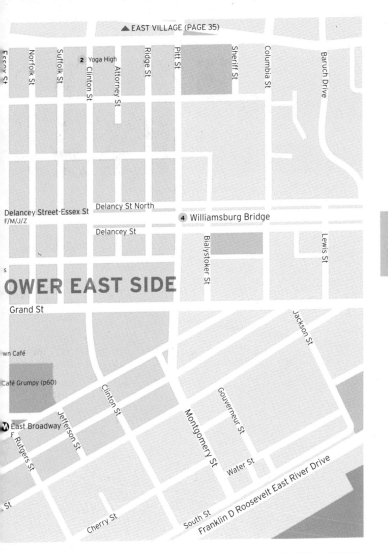

▲ EAST VILLAGE (PAGE 35)

Norfolk St

Suffolk St

2 Yoga High

Clinton St

Attorney St

Ridge St

Pitt St

Sheriff St

Columbia St

Baruch Drive

Essex St

Delancey Street-Essex St
F/M/J/Z

Delancy St North

Delancey St

4 Williamsburg Bridge

Bialystoker St

Lewis St

s

OWER EAST SIDE

Grand St

wn Café

Café Grumpy (p60)

Ⓜ East Broadway
F

Rutgers St

Jefferson St

Clinton St

Montgomery St

Gouverneur St

Water St

Jackson St

South St

Franklin D Roosevelt East River Drive

St

Cherry St

Cosmopolitan Brunch Spot

Brown Café

① 61 Hester St, between Ludlow St and Essex St
+1 212 477 2427
greenbrownorange.com
Ⓜ East Broadway Ⓕ, Delancey St-Essex St ⒻⓂⒿⓏ, Grand St ⒷⒹ
Open daily 9am-6pm. Dinner Fri 7pm-1am.

Nestled in an up-and-coming corner of Hester Street between Chinatown and the Lower East Side, Brown Café is an urban take on a log cabin. The café and its private next door dining room, Orange, exude natural warmth. Simple and delicious meals are prepared from locally sourced sustainable, free range and organic ingredients. The owner, Alejandro Alcocer, originally from Mexico City, built the wooden chairs and tables himself. The menu reflects his cosmopolitan flair.

Yoga Studio

Yoga High

② 19 Clinton St, #205, between East Houston St and Stanton St
+1 212 792 5776
yogahighnyc.com
Ⓜ Delancey St-Essex St ⒻⓂⒿⓏ
Classes daily. $20 per class or $16 for an express class; $2 mat rental; no showers on premises.

A fabulous independent yoga studio located atop lively Clinton Street. The studio retains a local vibe while maintaining a vibrant and cosmopolitan feel. Owners Mel Russo and Liz Buehler-Walker have hand selected the remaining instructors, making the uncompromising *vinyasa* pedagogy uniformly excellent. The space is spotless and soothing and feels like an urban retreat. After your *savasana*, you can pop down to Cocoa Bar next door for a dark chocolate infused rooibos tea or a glass of wine.

Synagogue & Museum

Eldridge St Synagogue

③ 12 Eldridge St, between Canal St and Division St
+1 212 219 0888
eldridgestreet.org
Ⓜ East Broadway **Ⓕ**, Grand St **ⒷⒹ**
Closed Sat. Open Sun-Thu 10am-5pm. Fri 10am-3pm. Admission $10.

The Eldridge Street Synagogue first opened its doors in 1887. The structure's opulent Moorish design and jewel like interior reflect the aspirations of the waves of Eastern European and Russian Jewish immigrants that formed a seminal part of the fabric of the 19th and early 20th century Lower East Side. In 2007, the synagogue was restored to its former glory, receiving several historical restoration awards, and is now open to the public as the Museum at Eldridge Street.

Engineering Marvel

East River Bridges

④ Across the East River, between Lower Manhattan and Brooklyn
Ⓜ Grand St **ⒷⒹ** (Manhattan Bridge), Delancey St-Essex St **ⒻⓂⒿⓏ** (Williamsburg Bridge), Brooklyn Bridge-City Hall/Chambers St **ⒿⓏ④** **⑤⑥** (Brooklyn Bridge)
Public access.

No other single structure is more emblematic of New York than the Brooklyn Bridge—a bold engineering feat, crossing a maritime strait, built by German-born immigrant John Augustus Roebling. Its early 20th century siblings, the Williamsburg Bridge and the Manhattan Bridge (pictured above), are no less impressive; the latter carrying seven lanes of traffic and four subway lines into Downtown Manhattan. All three bridges offer stunning views from their pedestrian walkways.

Design Classics

Project No. 8

⑤ 38 Orchard St, at Hester St
+1 212 925 5599
projectno8.com
Ⓜ East Broadway **Ⓕ**, Delancey St-
Essex St **ⒻⓂⒿⓏ**, Grand St **ⒷⒹ**
Open daily noon-7pm.

Located on an urban-edgy block
at the intersection of the Lower
East Side and Chinatown, Project
No. 8 features an arresting array of
men's fashion and other delectable
goods with a European bent.
Whether you're searching for
Kaweco fountain pens, men's luxury
underwear, a hand knit woolen
pigeon or a 1950s Braun desk
ventilator, Project No. 8 is sure to
please. A second outlet, located at
the Ace Hotel (p58), specializes in
travel goods.

Americana Brunch

Freemans

⑥ Freeman Alley, off Rivington St,
between Bowery and Chrystie St
+1 212 420 0012
freemansrestaurant.com
Ⓜ Bowery **ⒿⓏ**, 2 Av **Ⓕ**, Spring **Ⓖ**
Open daily. Dinner 6pm-11.30pm.
Lunch Mon-Fri 11am-4pm. Brunch
Sat/Sun 10am-4pm.

A trendy locavore enclave and
brunch classic at the back of an
alley off Rivington Street, Freeman's
spearheaded the New York
mixology craze when it opened in
2004 and remains at the forefront of
culinary trends. The restaurant's old
Americana bent is reflected in all
details, from the stuffed wild game
adorning the walls to the inventive
rustic menu featuring local New
York produce. The wine list includes
food-friendly old world bottles and
several organic and biodynamic
selections.

Cocina Estilo Libre

Rayuela

⑦ 165 Allen St, between Rivington St
and Stanton St
+1 212 253 8840
rayuelanyc.com
Ⓜ 2 Av Ⓕ, Delancey St-Essex St Ⓕ
ⓂⒿⓏ
Open daily. Dinner Mon-Thu 5.30pm-
11pm; Fri/Sat 5.30pm-midnight;
Sun 5pm-10pm. Brunch Sat/Sun
11am-4pm.

Furnished with its own in-house
tree, Rayuela stands for culinary
experimentation in a stylish setting.
The restaurant's name is derived
from the eponymous Julio Cortázar
novel, where chapters can be
read linearly or interchangeably—
"hopscotch" style. Accordingly,
executive chef Máximo Tejada
weaves "free style" Latin American
dishes from ingredients sourced
from across the region and Spain,
liberally mixing and matching
elements from regional cuisines
with refreshing results.

Pasta e Vino

Sorella

⑧ 95 Allen St, between Delancey St
and Broome St
+1 212 274 9595
sorellanyc.com
Ⓜ Grand St ⒷⒹ, Delancey St-Essex
St ⒻⓂⒿⓏ
Closed Mon. Open Tue-Sat 6pm-
2am; Sun 5.30pm-midnight.

Sorella is a Northern Italian inspired
establishment at the intersection of
Chinatown and the Lower East Side.
The restaurant's intricate facade
artfully conceals the convivial space
inside. This is a great spot for an
evening conversation over wine
and pasta in a decidedly downtown
setting. After dinner, drop by
Stellina, the sister gelateria next
door for desert.

Downtown Independent Film

Sunshine Cinema

9 143 East Houston St, between
Forsyth St and Eldridge St
+1 212 330 8182
landmarktheatres.com
M 2 Av **F**, Bowery **J Z**
Screenings daily. Refer to website
for showtimes. Tickets $13.

The Sunshine Cinema provides
a excellent locale for viewing
the latest independent and
international films in a plush and
contemporary setting. Boasting
five screens, the cinema also has a
café and an upstairs seating area
with views across bustling Houston
Street. The building itself, dating
from 1898, was once home to the
Houston Hippodrome cinema,
which later morphed into a Yiddish
vaudeville theatre and yet again
into a hardware storage facility.
The Landmark cinema group re-
engineered the space back into a
cinema in 2001.

Natural Wines & Tapas

The Ten Bells

10 247 Broome St, between Orchard
St and Ludlow St
+1 212 228 4450
thetenbells.com
M Delancey St-Essex St **F M J Z**,
Grand St **B D**
Open daily. Mon-Fri 5pm-2am; Sat/
Sun 3pm-2am.

Founded as a sustainable and
organic wine and small plates
bar in 2008, The Ten Bells takes
"low sulfite" to new heights. The
resulting collection of mostly
European bottles is daring and
unusual. The eclectic space is
designed as a cosy amalgam of
European wine cellar and typical
Lower East Side tenement-style
den, complete with pressed-tin
ceiling, votive candles, unreadable
chalk board, luscious blossom
arrangements and a luxurious slab
of a marble bar.

Chelsea & Flatiron

—Multilevel Gallery Land

Chelsea has long lived in the shadows cast by its star-studded downtown neighbours. However, the neighbourhood became popular with a more bohemian crowd, both gay and straight, as the West Village was discovered by the wealthy. On the far side of 8th Avenue, western Chelsea's industrial wasteland has transformed itself into gallery land, with a string of world class bijou art galleries (p59) popping up on and off 10th Avenue. The neighbourhood's far western reaches were finally made accessible to the general public in 2009 by the advent of the High Line (p60), an elevated park on former freight rail tracks. Chelsea's Far West has since developed into a showcase for Starchitect designed luxury apartment buildings.

To the east lies the Flatiron District, named after the famous Flatiron Building at 23rd Street and Broadway. The area was once home to New York's most notable department stores, but by the mid-20th century became dominated by clothing and toy manufacturers. Today, the Flatiron District has rediscovered its commercial roots and its stunning architecture is now home to numerous publishers and advertising agencies, as well as the core of "Silicon Alley", New York's thriving tech start-up scene.

The area north of Madison Square Park (or "NoMad") still has a distinctly 1980s New York feel to it, with wholesalers of jewellery and hair extensions pursuing their trades out of the lower floors of elegant late 19th century former hotels and office buildings.

Frankenthaler Motherwell
Rauschenberg Close
Warhol Thiebaud Kelly
Hewitt
Dine Kentridge

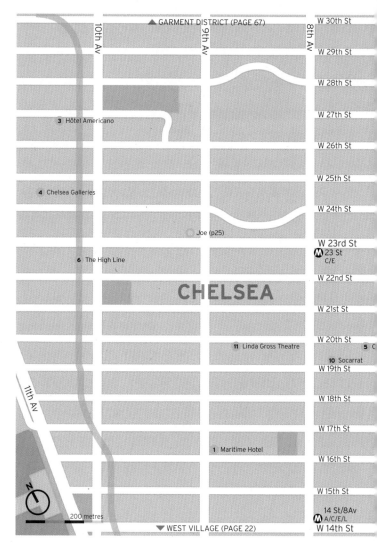

▲ GARMENT DISTRICT (PAGE 67)

W 30th St
W 29th St
W 28th St
W 27th St
W 26th St
W 25th St
W 24th St
W 23rd St
Ⓜ 23 St
C/E
W 22nd St
W 21st St
W 20th St
W 19th St
W 18th St
W 17th St
W 16th St
W 15th St
14 St/8Av
Ⓜ A/C/E/L
W 14th St

10th Av
9th Av
8th Av
11th Av

3 Hôtel Americano

4 Chelsea Galleries

Joe (p25)

6 The High Line

CHELSEA

11 Linda Gross Theatre

5 C

10 Socarrat

1 Maritime Hotel

N

200 metres

▼ WEST VILLAGE (PAGE 22)

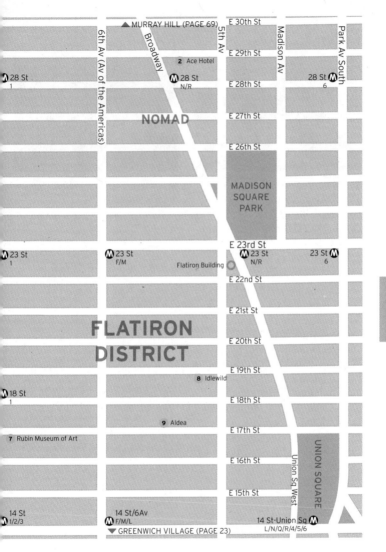

▲ MURRAY HILL (PAGE 69)

Broadway

6th Av (Av of the Americas)

5th Av

E 30th St

Madison Av

Park Av South

2 Ace Hotel

E 29th St

Ⓜ 28 St
1

Ⓜ 28 St
N/R

E 28th St

28 St Ⓜ
6

E 27th St

NOMAD

E 26th St

MADISON
SQUARE
PARK

E 23rd St

Ⓜ 23 St
1

Ⓜ 23 St
F/M

Ⓜ 23 St
N/R

23 St Ⓜ
6

Flatiron Building ○

E 22nd St

E 21st St

FLATIRON

E 20th St

DISTRICT

E 19th St

8 Idlewild

Ⓜ 18 St
1

E 18th St

9 Aldea

E 17th St

7 Rubin Museum of Art

E 16th St

UNION SQUARE

Union Sq West

E 15th St

14 St
Ⓜ 1/2/3

14 St/6Av
Ⓜ F/M/L

14 St-Union Sq Ⓜ
L/N/Q/R/4/5/6

▼ GREENWICH VILLAGE (PAGE 23)

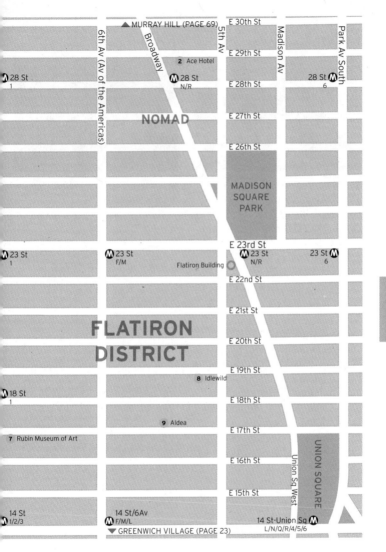

(map of Chelsea & Flatiron district)

- ▲ MURRAY HILL (PAGE 69)
- **2** Ace Hotel
- **NOMAD**
- MADISON SQUARE PARK
- Flatiron Building
- **FLATIRON DISTRICT**
- **8** Idlewild
- **9** Aldea
- **7** Rubin Museum of Art
- UNION SQUARE
- ▼ GREENWICH VILLAGE (PAGE 23)

Streets: E 30th St, E 29th St, E 28th St, E 27th St, E 26th St, E 23rd St, E 22nd St, E 21st St, E 20th St, E 19th St, E 18th St, E 17th St, E 16th St, E 15th St

Avenues: 6th Av (Av of the Americas), Broadway, 5th Av, Madison Av, Park Av South, Union Sq West

Subway stations:
- Ⓜ 28 St (1)
- Ⓜ 28 St (N/R)
- 28 St Ⓜ (6)
- Ⓜ 23 St (1)
- Ⓜ 23 St (F/M)
- Ⓜ 23 St (N/R)
- 23 St Ⓜ (6)
- Ⓜ 18 St (1)
- 14 St Ⓜ (1/2/3)
- 14 St/6Av Ⓜ (F/M/L)
- 14 St-Union Sq Ⓜ (L/N/Q/R/4/5/6)

Nautical Chelsea Hotel

Maritime Hotel

① 363 West 16th St, at 9th Av
+1 212 242 4300
themaritimehotel.com
Ⓜ 14 St/8 Av Ⓐ Ⓒ Ⓔ Ⓛ, 14 St ① ② ③,
Doubles from $319/night incl. tax;
excl. breakfast, available in-house.

Resembling a smart 1960s cruise
liner, replete with portholes and
deck bar, the Maritime is a unique
hotel that incorporates a certain
thrown-back-in-time flair. The
lobby lounge is the perfect spot
to relax by the crackling fire amid
the nautically inspired decoration,
luxurious marine blue carpet and
dark wooden panels. The hotel is a
world unto itself, allowing guests
to bathe in its tranquillity and rest
weary muscles after all that NYC
moving and shaking.

Flatiron Hotel

Ace Hotel

② 20 West 29th St, between
Broadway and 5th Av
+1 212 679 2222
acehotel.com
Ⓜ 28 St Ⓝ Ⓡ, 28 St ①, 28 St ⑥
Doubles from $347/night incl. tax;
bunkbed room from $301/night
incl. tax; excl. breakfast, available
in-house.

A Portland import, the Ace is at
once Macbook hipster hangout,
coffee connoisseur's den and
design executive's preferred
meeting spot. Located in the centre
of the newly fashionable "NoMad"
neighbourhood, the Ace remains
true to its Northwestern roots,
sporting heads of various wild
game on its walls and raw leather
sofas throughout its wooden
interior. The café is run by Portland
based roaster Stumptown, and the
hotel is constantly cracking with
media type creativity.

Amid the Galleries
Hôtel Americano

③ 518 West 27th St, between 10th Av and 11th Av
+1 212 216 0000
hotel-americano.com
Ⓜ 23 St **Ⓒ Ⓔ**
Doubles from $319/night incl. tax; excl. breakfast; available in-house.

Located in the core of the Chelsea gallery district within a stone's throw of the High Line, Mexican Grupo Habita's Hôtel Americano is slick, urbane and sophisticated. Amenities include a rooftop pool with cabanas, a Franco-Latin fusion restaurant and a futuristic bar. Decorated with simple lines and warm tones, rooms exude tranquillity, often deliciously juxtaposed with edgy Manhattan views. Capitalizing on the hotel's riparian location, guests can borrow bicycles to ride along the river on the Hudson River Greenway's bike path.

Gallery Land
Chelsea Galleries

④ West 20th St to West 27th St, between 10th Av and 11th Av
chelseagallerymap.com
Ⓜ 23 St **Ⓒ Ⓔ**
Most galleries typically open Tue-Sat 10am-6pm.

In Chelsea's far western reaches lies a unique assemblage of 350+ innovative art galleries, interwoven with cutting edge fashion boutiques, such as the tubular shaped local branch of Comme des Garçons. The galleries are notable for hosting shows by a panoply of modern and contemporary artists at the forefront of the global art scene. Of particular note are the Gagosian, Sean Kelly, and Pace Galleries, and the Chelsea Art Museum, which has an in-house café.

Coffee Boost

Café Grumpy

⑤ 224 West 20th St, between 7th Av and 8th Av

+1 212 255 5511

cafegrumpy.com

Ⓜ 23 St ⒸⒺ, 18 St ①

Open daily. Mon-Fri 7am-8pm; Sat 7.30am-8pm; Sun 7.30am-7.30pm.

Donning a scowl, this Chelsea haunt's cloud like logo welcomes you to a narrow, brightly colored interior dotted with plants. In spite of the café's name, the coffee at Grumpy is good enough to lift the spirits of even the surliest grouch. The outdoor benches on pretty 20th Street provide the ideal spot to socialize with the neighbourhood's well-heeled canine population and its posse of macchiato sipping owners.

Elevated Park

The High Line

⑥ Gansevoort St to West 30th St, near 10th Av

+1 212 500 6035

thehighline.org

Ⓜ 14 St/8 Av ⒶⒸⒺⓁ, 23 St ⒸⒺ

Open daily 7am-7pm. 9 stairways and elevators along the park.

The High Line is a throwback to Manhattan's industrial past, when adjacent warehouses were linked up to this unique elevated freight railroad. As the port moved to more spacious terrain across the river, the tracks lay obsolete for decades, overgrown with a distinctly urban vegetation of wild grasses and shrubs. Sticking out amid the Meatpacking District's contemporary retail frenzy, the High Line faced destruction before a compromise was reached to transform it into a park inspired by the self-seeded landscape that grew spontaneously along its tracks.

Museum of Tibetan Art
Rubin Museum of Art

7 150 West 17th St, between 6th
Avenue and 7th Avenue
+1 212 620 5000
rmanyc.org
Ⓜ 18 St ①, 14 St/6 Av Ⓕ Ⓜ Ⓛ
Closed Tue. Open Mon/Thu 11am-
5pm; Wed 11am-7pm; Fri 11am-10pm;
Sat/Sun 11am-6pm. Admission $10.

A tranquil spot to pop in for some
Himalayan lunch and/or artwork,
the Rubin Museum is a rather
atypical venue for a neighbourhood
commonly defined by its
contemporary design credentials.
The gallery holds regular talks
and screenings related to Tibetan
Art and Buddhism. Browse the
bookstore for specialist publications
on everything from yoga and
meditation to Tibetan artefacts.
Decorated in a mossy green and
replete with images of the Buddha,
the museum's café is a relaxing
lunch option.

Travel Bookshop
Idlewild

8 12 West 19th St, between 5th Av
and 6th Av
+1 212 414 8888
idlewildbooks.com
Ⓜ 23 St Ⓝ Ⓡ, 14 St/6 Av Ⓕ Ⓜ Ⓛ,
14 St-Union Sq Ⓛ Ⓝ Ⓠ Ⓡ ④ ⑤ ⑥
Open daily. Mon-Thu noon-7.30pm;
Fri-Sun noon-7pm.

Replete with an impressive
collection of globes, Idlewild is
a travel bookshop woven into
the fabric of the Flatiron District's
innumerable furniture design
and interior stores. Light and
comfortable, the bookshop allows
for ample armchair travel, covering
everything from foreign literature
to travel writing, cartography books
and a global selection of children's
classics. Idlewild also carries an
impressive array of titles in French,
Spanish and Italian and offers
language classes at both its Flatiron
and Brooklyn locations.

Elegant Iberian Restaurant

Aldea

9 31 West 17th St, between 5th Av and 6th Av

+1 212 675 7223

aldearestaurant.com

M 14 St/6 Av **F M L**, 14 St-Union Sq **L N Q R 4 5 6**, 18 St **1**

Open daily. Dinner Mon 5.30pm-10pm; Tue-Thu 5.30pm-11pm; Fri/Sat 5.30pm-midnight; Sun 5pm-9pm. Lunch Mon-Fri 11.30am-2pm.

Aldea's exclusive and serene design does not eschew underlying warmth. The sophisticated setting is underscored by muted tones and subtle but inventive dishes inspired by the culinary traditions of the Iberian Peninsula, supported by an intricate wine list. Inspired by a *stage* completed at Martin Berasategui in San Sebastian, celebrated Portuguese-American chef George Mendez embarked on this venture seeking to improvise on Iberian traditions and innovations. The results are enticing.

Paella Bar

Socarrat

10 259 West 19th St, between 7th Av and 8th Av

+1 212 462 1000

socarratpaellabar.com

M 18 St **1**, 14 St/8 Av **A C E L**

Open daily. Dinner Sun-Thu 5pm-11pm; Fri/Sat 5pm-midnight. Lunch daily noon-3pm.

Socarrat is a lively paella and tapas restaurant in the heart of Chelsea, the traditional home of New York's Spanish community. The space is divided into a restaurant, dominated by a long communal table, and a separate bar room, where a limited Tapas menu is available. Dark wood, frenetic conversation and a distinctly Spanish feel predominate. The crowds keep coming back for the scrumptious varieties of paella, classic tapas, such as *gambas al ajillo* and *patatas bravas*, solid Spanish wine list and decadent deserts and sherries.

Mamet's Theatre

Atlantic Theater Co.

⑪ Linda Gross Theater, 336 West
20th St, between 8th Av and 9th Av
+1 212 691 5919
atlantictheater.org

Ⓜ 23 St Ⓒ Ⓔ

Regular performances. Refer to
website for program.

At the forefront of the American
theatrical scene since its inception
in 1985, the Atlantic Theater Co.
doubles as a dramatic academy.
The company was founded by
celebrated playwright David Mamet
and Coen Brothers veteran William
H. Macy. Productions generally
comprise contemporary American
plays, including premieres of works
by Mamet and Sam Shepard. The
theatre's setting, in a converted
church on one of Chelsea's
historical seminary blocks, allows for
an invigorating pre-theatrical stroll
through the maze of art galleries
just across 9th Avenue.

Midtown

—New York City's Commercial Hub

Midtown constitutes the pulsating centre of the city where myriad high-rise office towers complement the Empire State and Chrysler Buildings to form New York's celebrated skyline. Midtown East, between 5th and Lexington Avenues, is a shopping paradise with department stores and boutiques catering to all tastes and wallets. Amidst the bustle, the stunning modernist architecture of Park Avenue, including Mies van der Rohe's Seagram Building, harkens back to the glamour of mid-century America.

Midtown's eastern fringes are home to the United Nations and several international cultural institutions, but otherwise largely residential. The Roosevelt Island cable car (p71), adjoining the Queensboro Bridge at 59th Street, offers spectacular views of the skyline and down the East River.

To the west, frenetic Times Square and the adjacent Theater District have developed into tourist hotspots with a distinctly commercial feel. Hell's Kitchen, Midtown's far west, attracts visitors and new residents with its eclectic range of small bars and restaurants thronging 9th Avenue and beyond.

Below 42nd Street, the Garment District's busy wheeling and dealing stands in contrast to the orchestrated retail experience usually associated with Midtown. Korea Town (p76), the commercial and social focus of New York's large Korean community, is just around the corner from the Empire State Building.

MIDTOWN WEST

MIDTOWN EAST (PAGE 68)

THEATER DISTRICT

HELL'S KITCHEN

CENTRAL PARK

UPPER WEST SIDE (PAGE 80)

59 St-Columbus Circle
A/C/B/D/1

57 St
N/Q/R

7 Av
B/D/E

49 St
N/R

50 St
1

50 St
C/E

7th Av

Broadway

8th Av

9th Av

10th Av

11th Av

12th Av

W 60th St

W 59th St

W 58th St

W 57th St

W 56th St

W 55th St

W 54th St

W 53rd St

W 52nd St

W 51st St

W 50th St

W 49th St

W 48th St

W 47th St

W 46th St

10 Alvin Ailey

14 Casellula

15 Ardesia

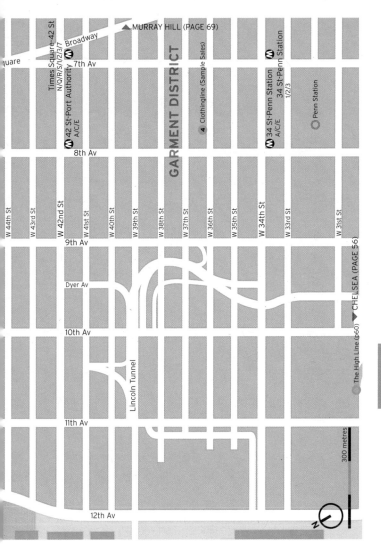

▲ MURRAY HILL (PAGE 69)

Times Square-42 St

Broadway

Times Square ❶ N/Q/R/S/1/2/3/7

7th Av

42 St-Port Authority
❷ A/C/E

34 St-Penn Station

34 St-Penn Station
❶ 34 St-Penn Station
A/C/E

1/2/3

○ Penn Station

GARMENT DISTRICT

❹ Clothingline (Sample Sales)

8th Av

W 44th St
W 43rd St
W 42nd St
W 41st St
W 40th St
W 39th St
W 38th St
W 37th St
W 36th St
W 35th St
W 34th St
W 33rd St
W 31st St

9th Av

Dyer Av

CHELSEA (PAGE 56) ▼

The High Line (p60) ○

10th Av

Lincoln Tunnel

11th Av

300 metres

12th Av

N

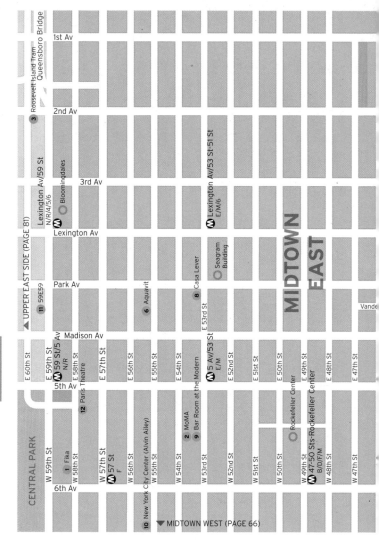

CENTRAL PARK

1st Av

Roosevelt Island Tram
Queensboro Bridge

2nd Av

3 Lexington Av/59 St
N/R/4/5/6

Bloomingdales

3rd Av

Lexington Av/53 St-51 St
E/M/6

Lexington Av

MIDTOWN

EAST

Seagram
Building

Casa Lever 8

Park Av

6 Aquavit

11 59E59

▲ UPPER EAST SIDE (PAGE 81)

Vande

E 53rd St

Madison Av

E 60th St
E 59th St
59 St/5 Av
N/R
E 58th St
Paris Theatre 12
E 57th St
E 56th St
E 55th St
E 54th St
5 Av/53 St
E/M
E 52nd St
E 51st St
E 50th St
E 49th St
E 48th St
E 47th St

5th Av

1 Fika

W 59th St
W 58th St

57 St
F

W 57th St
W 56th St

10 New York City Center (Alvin Ailey)

W 55th St
W 54th St

2 MoMA
9 Bar Room at the Modern

W 53rd St
W 52nd St
W 51st St

Rockefeller Center

W 50th St
W 49th St

47-50 Sts-Rockefeller Center
B/D/F/M

W 48th St
W 47th St

6th Av

▼ MIDTOWN WEST (PAGE 66)

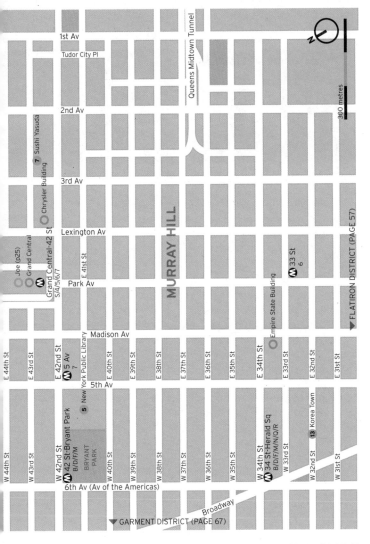

1st Av

Tudor City Pl

Queens Midtown Tunnel

2nd Av

7 Sushi Yasuda

Chrysler Building

3rd Av

MURRAY HILL

Lexington Av

Joe (p25)

Grand Central

Ⓜ Grand Central-42 St
S/4/5/6/7

E 41st St

Park Av

Ⓜ 33 St
6

Empire State Building

▶ FLATIRON DISTRICT (PAGE 57)

Madison Av

E 44th St

E 43rd St

Ⓜ E 42nd St
5 Av
7

5 New York Public Library

E 40th St

E 39th St

E 38th St

E 37th St

E 36th St

E 35th St

E 34th St

E 33rd St

E 32nd St

E 31st St

5th Av

W 44th St

W 43rd St

Ⓜ W 42nd St
42 St-Bryant Park
B/D/F/M

BRYANT PARK

W 40th St

W 39th St

W 38th St

W 37th St

W 36th St

W 35th St

Ⓜ W 34th St
34 St-Herald Sq
B/D/F/M/N/Q/R

W 33rd St

13 Korea Town

W 32nd St

W 31st St

6th Av (Av of the Americas)

Broadway

▼ GARMENT DISTRICT (PAGE 67)

300 metres

Swedish Coffee & Pick-Me-Up

Fika

① 41 West 58th St, between 5th Av and 6th Av
+1 212 832 0022
fikanyc.com
Ⓜ 57 St Ⓕ, 5 Av/59 St Ⓝ Ⓡ
Open daily. Mon-Fri 7am-7pm; Sat 9am-4pm; Sun 10am-4pm.

This Swedish coffee mini-chain has taken Manhattan by storm, populating the financial districts in Mid- and Downtown with the first real alternative to Starbucks. The store's decor is Scandinavian minimalist and designed to give the local business population a quick boost before returning to work. Black and white photographs of Stockholm adorn the walls, while fresh baked Swedish-style cinnamon buns (*kanelbulle*) and Scandinavian open faced *smörgåsar* await the lucky customer at the front till.

Museum of Modern Art

MoMA

② 11 West 53rd St, between 5th Av and 6th Av
+1 212 708 9400
moma.org
Ⓜ 5 Av/53 St Ⓔ Ⓜ, 7 Av Ⓑ Ⓓ Ⓔ
Closed Tue. Open Sat-Mon/Wed/Thu 10.30am-5.30pm; Fri 10.30am-8pm. Admission $25.

MoMA's innovative shows and expansive permanent collection encompassing 150,000 masterpieces place the museum at the forefront of the modern art world. Founded by Abby Rockefeller, wife of John D., against the latter's will, the museum gained iconic status through its Van Gogh and Picasso exhibitions in the 1930s. MoMA's multi-departmental structure includes sections devoted to architecture and design, film, video and photography, painting, sculpture, drawings and prints.

Tram over the East River

Roosevelt Island Tram

3 2nd Av, between East 59th St and East 60th St

Ⓜ Lexington Av/59 St **Ⓝ Ⓡ ④ ⑤ ⑥**, Lexington Av/63 St **Ⓕ**, Roosevelt Island **Ⓕ**

Operates daily. Sun-Thu 6am-2am; Fri/Sat 6am-3.30am. Tickets $2.50 each way; included in Metrocard.

The Roosevelt Island Tram provides a spectacular commuting option into Manhattan for the denizens of small Roosevelt Island. Owing to its isolated location in the East River, Roosevelt Island was the site of a prison and an insane asylum for much of its history. This changed in the 1970s when the island was opened up for residential development. The tramway was constructed as a temporary measure, but its popularity with residents and visitors alike has since made it a permanent fixture.

Fashion Sales

Sample Sales

4 261 West 36th St, between 7th Av and 8th Av

+1 212 947 8748

clothingline.com

Ⓜ 34 St-Penn Station **Ⓐ Ⓒ Ⓔ**, 34 St-Penn Station **① ② ③**

Open typically 11am-7pm. Refer to website for upcoming sales.

Relish in the city's fashion scene by engaging in a little discount retail therapy in the heart of the Garment District. Though lacking the customer service frills of the traditional retail experience, sample sales allow patrons to indulge in the guerilla warfare of designer purchases at massive discounts. Sizes are often thrown together, making the experience as much a treasure hunt as a shopping experience. Whilst most sample sales pop up overnight, Clothingline is a reliable purveyor of regular sales.

Glamorous Public Library

NY Public Library

Swedish Dining

Aquavit

⑤ 5th Av, between West 40th St and West 42nd St
+1 917 275 6975
nypl.org
Ⓜ 5 Av **❼**, 42 St-Bryant Park **Ⓑ Ⓓ Ⓕ Ⓜ**, Grand Central-42 St **Ⓢ ❹ ❺ ❻ ❼**
Open daily. Mon/Thu-Sat 10am-6pm; Tue/Wed 10am-8pm; Sun 1pm-5pm.

The New York Public Library's main Bryant Park branch houses an elegant Beaux-Arts maze of corridors and stunningly decorated hidden rooms. The library's gargantuan Rose Main Reading Room is worth a visit in of itself. Adjacent Bryant Park, furnished with movable chairs and tables during the warmer months, offers a green break from the Midtown buzz.

⑥ 65 East 55th St, between Madison Av and Park Av
+1 212 307 7311
aquavit.org
Ⓜ Lexington Av/53 St-51 St **Ⓔ Ⓜ ❻**, Lexington Av/59 St **Ⓝ Ⓡ ❹ ❺ ❻**
Closed Sun. Dinner Mon-Sat 5.30pm-10.30pm. Lunch Mon-Fri 11.45am-2.30pm.

A welcome change from the high octane Midtown dining scene, Aquavit serves up a smorgasbord of delightful Scandinavian cuisine. The front room bistro excels at unfussy, seasonal Nordic dishes ranging from the delectable herring sampler to the Arctic Circle parfait, while the dining room offers a comprehensive *prix fixe* menu. Relax at the bar, where you can enjoy your cured *gravlax* with a glass or two of champers.

Sushi par Excellence
Sushi Yasuda

⑦ 204 East 43rd St, between 2nd Av
and 3rd Av
+1 212 972 1001
sushiyasuda.com
Ⓜ Grand Central-42 St ⑤④⑤⑥⑦
Closed Sun. Dinner Mon-Sat 6pm-
10.15pm. Lunch Mon-Fri noon-2.15pm.

Arguably the best purveyor of sushi
in New York City, Yasuda settles
for nothing short of excellence.
From the imposing wooden sushi
counter, where you can order
an *omakase* nonstop succession
of delights, to the resolutely
minimalist yet warm interior, every
detail is meticulously executed.
The lunch and dinner sushi sets
are particularly enjoyable, as
the chef will point out the day's
freshest ingredients for you to
select from. Wherever possible,
fish is locally sourced. A top-
notch comprehensive sake list
complements the menu.

Warhol & Pasta
Casa Lever

⑧ 390 Park Av, at East 53rd St
+1 212 888 2700
casalever.com
Ⓜ Lexington Av/53 St-51 St ⒺⓂ⑥
Closed Sun. Open Mon-Fri 7am-11pm;
Sat 11am-11pm.

Housed in the iconic Lever House
and exquisitely designed in Milan-
meets-Manhattan 1970s retro-
splendour, Casa Lever's power set
clientele is offset by the bonhomie
of the establishment's Italian staff.
The extensive Northern Italian
menu is carefully prepared and
includes such delicacies as *tagliata
di bufalo* and *pappardelle* in slow
cooked duck ragu. A celebratory
space, with a gorgeous marble clad
front bar, crystal chandeliers and
nineteen oversized Warhol portraits,
the environment never fails to
inspire.

Urbane Bar and Brasserie

Bar Room at The Modern

⑨ 9 West 53rd St, between 5th Av and 6th Av
+1 212 333 1220
themodernnyc.com
Ⓜ 5 Av/53 St ❸ Ⓜ, 7 Av ❸ ❹ ❺
Open daily. Mon-Thu 11.30am-10.30pm; Fri/Sat 11.30am-11pm; Sun 11.30am-9.30pm.

Set within the cultural mecca of MoMA (p70), the Bar Room at The Modern exudes sophisticated ease. Both opulent and modernist in feel, the bar offers a comprehensive wine and cocktail list and a range of Alsatian inspired dishes. This is one of the rare places where cultural and business world types sip side by side. We recommend you slip off to the Bar Room after a visit to MoMA to indulge in a glass of Lucien Albrecht's high calibre *Crémant d'Alsace* as a cultural aperitif.

American Modern Dance

Alvin Ailey

⑩ 405 West 55th St, at 9th Av
+1 212 581 1212
alvinailey.org
Ⓜ 59 St-Columbus Circle Ⓐ Ⓒ Ⓑ Ⓓ ❶
Regularly performing at New York City Center (130 West 56th Street) when not touring. Tickets from $25.

Perhaps nothing captures NYC's energy better than Alvin Ailey's American Dance Theater. Founded in the city in 1958, it has played a seminal role in both the American and global modern dance scene ever since. Fusing elements of ballet, modern, jazz and African dance, the company's riveting choreography remains distinctly path breaking. Classics such as *Revelations*, Ailey's 1960 signature piece, are regularly performed alongside more recent innovations. The company also offers dance classes at all levels at its studio overlooking the Midtown cityscape.

Off-Broadway Theatre

59E59

⓫ 59 East 59th St, between Madison Av and Park Av
+1 212 753 5959
59e59.org
Ⓜ 5 Av/59 St Ⓝ Ⓡ, Lexington Av/59 St Ⓝ Ⓡ ④⑤⑥, Lexington Av/63 St Ⓕ
Regular performances. Refer to website for program.

Housing three stages and a convivial 2nd floor bar, the 59E59 Theater presents an eclectic selection of Off-Broadway plays safely positioned across town from the overly worn dancing feet of West 42nd Street. Launched in 2002 as a venue to showcase work by up-and-coming playwrights, the theatre stages productions by its resident company, Primary Stages, and also hosts visiting companies. The cracking "Brits off Broadway" festival, held each fall, is a particular draw.

Historic Cinema

Paris Theatre

⓬ 4 West 58th St, between 5th Av and 6th Av
+1 212 688 3800
theparistheatre.com
Ⓜ 5 Av/59 St Ⓝ Ⓡ, 57 St Ⓕ
Screenings daily. Refer to website for showtimes. Tickets $13.

An elegant single screen movie theatre opened in 1948 by the French Pathé cinema group, the Paris Theatre maintains much of its original Continental flair. Marlene Dietrich cut the inaugural ribbon on opening night. The cinema has a history of screening art house, international and independent films to a discerning crowd, and the location, across the street from Bergdorf Goodman, the Plaza Hotel and Central Park (p86) is literally in the middle of it all.

Commerce & Entertainment

Korea Town

⓭ West 32nd St, between Broadway and 5th Av

Ⓜ 34 St-Herald Sq Ⓑ Ⓓ Ⓕ Ⓜ Ⓝ Ⓠ Ⓡ, 33 St ⑥

Public access. Cho Dang Gol: open daily 11.30am-11pm.

New York is home to one of the largest ethnic Korean populations outside Korea and "K-Town" is at its epicentre. Home to only a small Korean resident population, the streets around 32nd Street, between 5th Avenue and Broadway, are primarily a business and entertainment district. Some buildings boast multiple storeys of Korean businesses, including banks and beauty parlours, karaoke lounges and restaurants—among which Cho Dang Gol, a few blocks up on 35th Street, has established itself as a popular dining option.

Wine and Cheese Bar

Casellula

⓮ 401 West 52nd St, between 9th Av and 10th Av

+1 212 247 8137

casellula.com

Ⓜ 50 St Ⓒ Ⓔ, 59 St-Columbus Circle Ⓐ Ⓒ Ⓑ Ⓓ ❶

Open daily 5pm-2am.

A Hell's Kitchen stalwart, Casellula is predominantly an artisanal wine and cheese bar, but also carries a host of smoked meats to accompany the 40+ international varieties of cheese. Located on a pleasant stretch of 52nd Street and decked out with a thick wooden plank floor, Casellula reveals a more serene, quality driven facet of a neighbourhood still dominated by fast food joints and tourist haunts. Reservations are not taken, so try to arrive early or expect a bit of a wait.

Hell's Kitchen Wine Bar

Ardesia

⑮ 510 West 52nd St, between 10th
Av and 11th Av
+1 212 247 9191
ardesia-ny.com
Ⓜ 50 St **ⒸⒺ**, 59 St-Columbus Circle
ⒶⒸⒷⒹ①
Open daily. Mon-Wed 5pm-midnight;
Thu/Fri 5pm-2am; Sat 5pm-2am;
Sun 5pm-11pm.

A happy medium between Hell's
Kitchen's semi-edgy throngs and
Columbus Circle's preppy crowd,
Ardesia provides a modern setting
accentuated by cool tones and a
comfortable lounge section. The
wine list is top-notch, extensive and
unusual. The food menu includes
innovative takes on international
small plates, as well as several
classics. This is the perfect spot to
enjoy a glass of cava and a spate
of olives and crostini before a
performance at the nearby Lincoln
Center (p87).

Uptown

—Manhattan's High-Rise Suburbs

The Upper East Side is the traditional abode of New York's established wealth and social life, with consulates occupying generous townhouses and exclusive boutiques lining Madison Avenue. The neighbourhood is also the site of most of New York's world class museums, including the Metropolitan Museum of Art and the Guggenheim (p84); many of them located just across Central Park, along Fifth Avenue.

The Upper West Side, considered less sophisticated by New York's East Side establishment, is the preferred domicile of families and young professionals. Despite its busy Midtown feel around Columbus Circle and the Lincoln Center (p87), the neighbourhood's epicentre around 72nd Street is mostly residential, with attractive brownstone townhouses flanking leafy streets.

Harlem is arguably the most distinct of Manhattan's uptown neighbourhoods. Built as the borough's first "suburb" in a late 19th century property boom, the area became the centre of African American culture during the 1920s Harlem Renaissance. With the end of prohibition and the advent of the Great Depression, the neighbourhood experienced a reversal of fortune, and by the mid-20th century Harlem had become synonymous with urban blight. However, since the 2000s, the area has experienced something of a second renaissance, bolstered by an ethnically mixed demographic of young professionals attracted to the handsome brownstone blocks around Marcus Garvey Park.

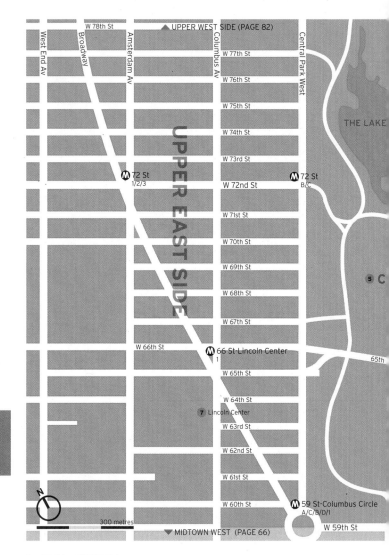

▲ UPPER WEST SIDE (PAGE 82)

THE LAKE

UPPER EAST SIDE

West End Av
Broadway
Amsterdam Av
Columbus Av
Central Park West

W 78th St
W 77th St
W 76th St
W 75th St
W 74th St
W 73rd St
Ⓜ 72 St
1/2/3
W 72nd St
Ⓜ 72 St
B/C
W 71st St
W 70th St
W 69th St
W 68th St
W 67th St
W 66th St
Ⓜ 66 St-Lincoln Center
1
W 65th St
W 64th St
7 Lincoln Center
W 63rd St
W 62nd St
W 61st St
W 60th St
Ⓜ 59 St-Columbus Circle
A/C/B/D/1
W 59th St

5 C

65th

300 metres

▼ MIDTOWN WEST (PAGE 66)

▲ UPPER EAST SIDE (PAGE 83)

5th Av

Madison Av

E 77th St

Park Av

E 78th St

Ⓜ 77 St
6

3rd Av

Lexington Av

E 76th St

E 75th St

2 Whitney

● Joe (p25)

E 74th St

UPPER WEST SIDE

E 73rd St

E 72nd St

E 71st St

3 Frick Collection

E 70th St

E 69th St

L PARK

E 68th St

Ⓜ 68 St-Hunter College
6

E 67th St

E 66th St

E 65th St

E 64th St

Ⓜ Lexington Av/63 St
F

E 63rd St

E 62nd St

E 61st St

E 60th St

Ⓜ Lexington Av/59 St
N/R/4/5/6

E 59th St

AMBLE

▼ MIDTOWN EAST (PAGE 68)

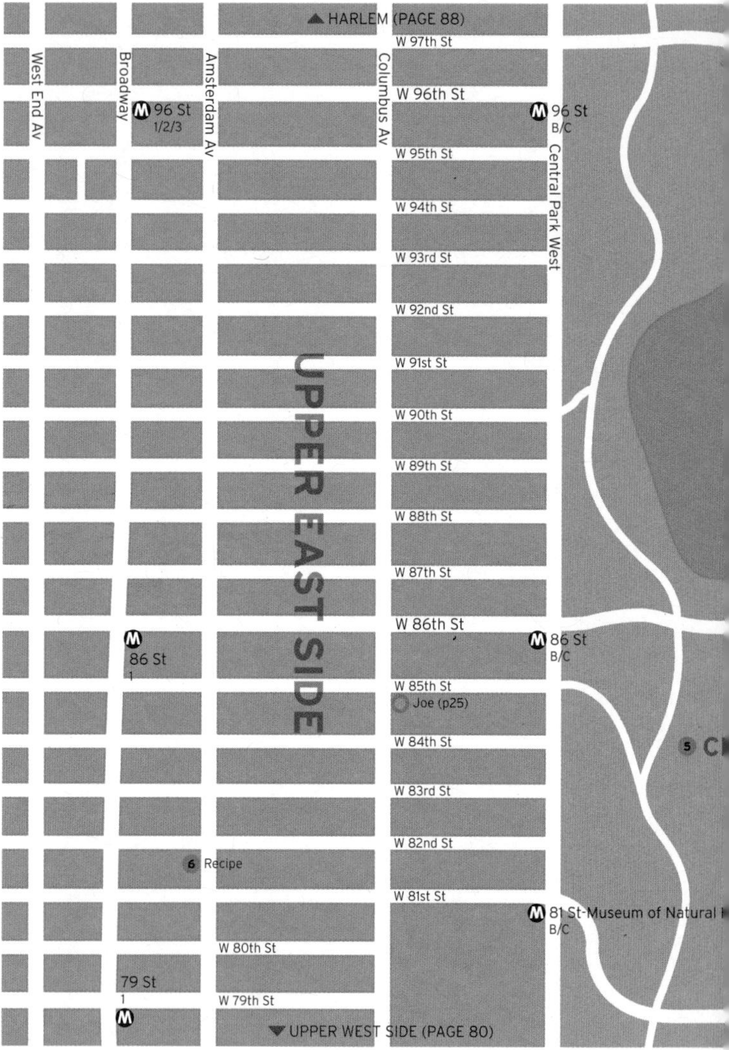

▲ HARLEM (PAGE 88)

West End Av

Broadway

Amsterdam Av

Columbus Av

Central Park West

W 97th St

W 96th St

Ⓜ 96 St
1/2/3

Ⓜ 96 St
B/C

W 95th St

W 94th St

W 93rd St

W 92nd St

W 91st St

W 90th St

W 89th St

W 88th St

W 87th St

W 86th St

UPPER EAST SIDE

Ⓜ 86 St
1

Ⓜ 86 St
B/C

W 85th St
◯ Joe (p25)

W 84th St

W 83rd St

W 82nd St

6 Recipe

W 81st St

Ⓜ 81 St-Museum of Natural H
B/C

W 80th St

79 St
1

W 79th St

Ⓜ

▼ UPPER WEST SIDE (PAGE 80)

5 Ⓒ

▲ HARLEM (PAGE 89)

Transverse

5th Av

Madison Av

Park Av

Ⓜ 96 St
6

Lexington Av

3rd Av

E 97th St

E 96th St

E 95th St

E 94th St

E 93rd St

E 92nd St

E 91st St

E 90th St

E 89th St

E 88th St

E 87th St

E 86th St **Ⓜ 86 St**
4/5/6

E 85th St

E 84th St

E 83rd St

E 82nd St

E 81st St

E 80th St

E 79th St

DELINE KENNEDY
SSIS RESERVOIR

ansverse

L PARK

sverse

UPPER WEST SIDE

1 Guggenheim

4 Neue Galerie

○ Metropolitan Museum of Art

300 metres

N

▼ UPPER EAST SIDE (PAGE 81)

Design Classic

Guggenheim

Modern American Art

Whitney

① 1071 5th Av, between East 88th St and East 89th St
+1 212 423 3500
guggenheim.org
Ⓜ 86 St **④⑤⑥**
Closed Thu. Open Sun-Wed/Fri 10am-5.45pm; Sat 10am-7.45pm. Admission $18.

The iconic Guggenheim Museum would be worth a visit simply for a glimpse at the rotundity of its mid-20th century architectural splendour. From within and without, Frank Lloyd Wright's luscious snail of a building maintains its original 1950s vitality. Engaging exhibitions featuring the world's top modern artists, curated to dot the structure's vertiginous walls, give art lovers good cause to return again and again.

② 945 Madison Av, at East 75th St
+1 212 570 3600
whitney.org
Ⓜ 77 St **⑥**
Closed Mon/Tue. Open Wed/Thu/Sat/Sun 11am-6pm; Fri 1pm-9pm. Admission $18.

In the Greenwich Village of the 1910s, sculptress and patron of the arts Gertrude Vanderbilt Whitney developed a contemporary *Salon des Refusés*, providing a showcase for disregarded contemporary American artists whose work she advocated. In 1931, she embarked on her own gallery venture. Following its original mandate, the Whitney exhibits modern and contemporary American artists' work. The museum's extensive permanent collection includes works by Edward Hopper, Jasper Johns, Georgia O'Keiffe and Jackson Pollock.

Industrialist & Collector's Home

Frick Collection

3 1 East 70th St, at 5th Av
+1 212 288 0700
frick.org
M 68 St-Hunter College **6**
Closed Mon. Open Tue-Sat 10am-6pm; Sun 11am-5pm. Admission $18.

Henry Clay Frick's outstanding art collection, including celebrated works by El Greco, Vermeer and Rembrandt, just to name a few, is on display at this 19th century Pittsburgh industrialist's palatial New York residence. Beyond the stunning collection, the mansion itself adds another dimension by offering insight into upper class New York life at the turn of the 20th century.

Mitteleuropa Art & Café Culture

Neue Galerie

4 1048 5th Av, at East 86th St
+1 212 628 6200
neuegalerie.org
M 86 St **456**
Closed Tue/Wed. Open Thu-Mon 11am-6pm. Admission $20. Café Sabarsky: Mon/Wed 9am-6pm; Thu-Sun 9am-9pm.

Housed in an elegant Upper East Side mansion by the park, the Neue Galerie's setting stands up to its refined, complex content. The brainchild of art-loving businessman Ronald S. Lauder and art dealer Serge Sabarsky, the museum houses a selective but categorical cross section of early 20th century German and Austrian art. Elegant Café Sabarsky and contemporary Viennese-style Café Fledermaus are both excellent spots to indulge in a slice of *Sachertorte* or a decanter of *Blaufränkisch*.

Manhattan's Green Lung

Central Park

⑤ Bordered clockwise by 110th St, 5th Av, Central Park South (59th St) and Central Park West (8th Av)
+1 212 310 6600
centralparknyc.org
Ⓜ 81 St-Museum of Natural History Ⓑ Ⓒ (for the Ramble), 72 St Ⓑ Ⓒ
Open daily 6am-1am.

Skyscrapers reaching over the dense foliage and vast lawns of Central Park are a defining feature of today's New York. However, the park was not actually contemplated when the city's famous street grid was laid out. The need for more urban greenspace became self-evident when 19th century New Yorkers had to take recourse to cemeteries for repose. Today, the park's southern reaches are a popular lunch break and tourist destination. Further north, the rocky elevations of the Ramble and beyond have a more natural feel.

Farm to Table Dining

Recipe

⑥ 452 Amsterdam Av, between West 81th St and West 82th St
+1 212 501 7755
recipenyc.com
Ⓜ 79 St ❶, 81 St-Museum of Natural History Ⓑ Ⓒ
Open daily. Dinner Mon-Thu/Sun 5pm-10.30pm; Fri/Sat 5pm-11.30pm. Brunch Sat/Sun 11am-3.30pm.

A small haven in the Upper West Side, Recipe's cosy twenty-six seat exposed brick interior provides the perfect setting for a casual sit down meal. The focus is on fresh, local and seasonal cuisine, and the menu varies according to what's currently available at market. Oven roasted whole Cornish hen, New York strip steak and risotto verde are but a few of the delightful mains that await the brunch or dinner guest.

World Class Performing Arts
Lincoln Center

⑦ 70 Lincoln Center Plaza, between West 62th St and West 66th St
+1 212 721 6500 (for tickets)
lincolncenter.org
Ⓜ 66 St-Lincoln Center ①, 59 St-Columbus Circle Ⓐ ⒸⒷⒹ①
Daily performances. Refer to website for program.

One of the world's premier performing arts venues, Lincoln Center comprises several top-flight resident companies, including the Metropolitan Opera, the New York City Ballet and the New York Philharmonic. An excellent film centre and the celebrated Juilliard School of Music are also housed in the complex. Visitors to the Met can relish in the splendour of the larger than life murals by Marc Chagall and chandeliers that float up into the ceiling at the beginning of any operatic performance.

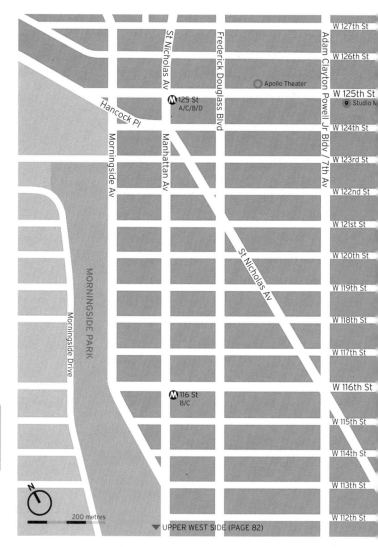

W 127th St
W 126th St
W 125th St
W 124th St
W 123rd St
W 122nd St
W 121st St
W 120th St
W 119th St
W 118th St
W 117th St
W 116th St
W 115th St
W 114th St
W 113th St
W 112th St

St Nicholas Av
Frederick Douglass Blvd
Adam Clayton Powell Jr Bldv / 7th Av
Hancock Pl
Morningside Av
Manhattan Av
St Nicholas Av
Morningside Drive

MORNINGSIDE PARK

Apollo Theater

Ⓜ 125 St
A/C/B/D

9 Studio M

Ⓜ 116 St
B/C

N

200 metres

▼ UPPER WEST SIDE (PAGE 82)

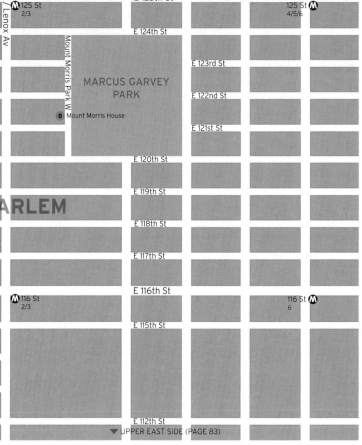

E 127th St

5th Av

Madison Av

Park Av

Lexington Av

E 126th St

Malcolm X Blvd / Lenox Av

10 Red Rooster

E 125th St

Ⓜ 125 St
2/3

125 St Ⓜ
4/5/6

E 124th St

Mount Morris Park W

E 123rd St

MARCUS GARVEY
PARK

E 122nd St

8 Mount Morris House

E 121st St

E 120th St

E 119th St

ARLEM

E 118th St

E 117th St

E 116th St

Ⓜ 116 St
2/3

116 St Ⓜ
6

E 115th St

E 112th St

▼ UPPER EAST SIDE (PAGE 83)

Harlem Renaissance B&B

Mount Morris House

⑧ 12 Mount Morris Park West, at West 121th St
+1 917 478 6214
mountmorrishouse.com
Ⓜ 125 St ❷❸, 125 St ❹❺❻
Doubles from $204/night incl. tax; breakfast included.

Housed in a gorgeous 1888 multilevel brownstone rising over Marcus Garvey Park (formerly Mount Morris Park), this historic B&B is a real home away from home. Guests stay in one of the house's beautifully appointed en-suite rooms, faithfully decorated with 19th century aplomb, without eschewing any of the modern comforts. Daily breakfast is served and the owners, who undertook much of the house's restoration work themselves, live on-site and are available to answer any questions about the city and Harlem.

Harlem Art Scene

Studio Museum

⑨ 144 West 125th St, between Malcolm X Boulevard and Adam Clayton Powell Jr. Boulevard
+1 212 864 4500
studiomuseum.org
Ⓜ 125 St ❷❸, 125 St Ⓐ ⒸⒷⒹ
Open Thu-Sun. Thu/Fri noon-9pm; Sat 10am-6pm; Sun noon-6pm. Admission $7.

The Studio Museum opened in 1968 as has since provided a platform for African American and African Art in New York City. The museum's artist in residence program has helped launch the careers of over 100 young artists, whose work is regularly showcased alongside that of artists at the forefront of their craft. The museum plays an integral part of the local cultural scene and is just a stroll away from the renowned Apollo Theater.

Contemporary Harlem Society

Red Rooster

🔟 310 Malcolm X Boulevard,
between W 125th St and W 126th St
+1 212 792 9001
redroosterharlem.com
Ⓜ 125 St ②③, 125 St ⒶⒸⒷⒹ
Open daily. Dinner Mon-Thu 5.30pm-
10.30pm; Fri-Sat 5.30pm-11.30pm;
Sun 5pm-10pm. Lunch Mon-Fri
11.30am-3pm. Brunch Sat/Sun 10am-
3pm.

Swedish-Ethiopian chef and
restaurateur Marcus Samuelsson
offers a felicitous interpretation of
organic farm to table cuisine of the
American South at his splendid
Harlem restaurant. The elegant
and upbeat front bar buzzes
with energy, while the dining
room in the back exudes a warm
contemporary flair. Thick wooden
bookshelves spill over with volumes
on Harlem's architecture and
multifaceted history.

Brooklyn
—The Other New York

Brooklyn was once a prosperous city in its own right—the fourth largest in the country—when it was consolidated into New York City in 1898. Today the most populous of the five New York boroughs, Brooklyn has retained a distinct social and cultural life, arguably more North American in feel than cosmopolitan Manhattan. Brooklyn's civic institutions, like the Brooklyn Academy of Music (p102), rank among the best and most respected in New York and beyond. Many of its neighbourhoods offer prime examples of the city's typical brownstone architecture.

Cobble Hill, Boerum Hill and Brooklyn Heights are elegantly leafy brownstone neighbourhoods, the latter offering panoramic views of the Manhattan skyline from its Promenade. Culturally vibrant Fort Greene and Clinton Hill boast stunning brownstone architecture, especially around Fort Greene Park. Downtown Brooklyn, still punctuated by throngs of parking lots, is in the fledgling stages of sprucing up to its former glory. Carroll Gardens, located further south along Smith and Court Streets, has maintained some of its Italian immigrant character.

Further south along Flatbush Avenue and adjacent to Prospect Park, sedate Park Slope and youthful Prospect Heights have established reputations for the diversity and sophistication of their café culture and poetry reading type residents.

A world apart from the rest of Brooklyn, Williamsburg and adjacent Greenpoint ostensibly host the largest number of hipsters in the world. The 20- and 30-something trendy residents populate an ever growing throng of *nouveau* speakeasies, seriously demanding eyewear boutiques and second hand just-about-everything stores.

▲ FORT GREENE (PAGE 96)

DUMBO

DOWNTOWN

BROOKLYN HEIGHTS

VINEGAR HILL

NAVY YARD

EAST RIVER

Manhattan Bridge

Brooklyn Bridge

Brooklyn Queens Expressway

▲ PARK SLOPE (PAGE 97)

Nevins St

BOERUM HILL

GOWANUS

Bond St

Hoyt St

Carroll St

Smith St

State St

Atlantic Av

Pacific St

Dean St

Bergen St

Bergen St
F/G

Wyckoff St

Warren St

10 Char No.4

Baltic St

Butler St

Douglass St

Degraw St

Sackett St

Union St

President St

Carroll Gardens
F/G

Carroll St

1st St

2nd St

3rd St

COBBLE HILL

Idlewild (p61)

CARROLL GARDENS

Tompkins Pl

2nd Pl

m Pl

art St

5 Colonie

Clinton St

6 Hibino

Strong Pl

Carroll St

1st Pl

Pl

St

Henry St

Amity St

Congress St

Warren St

Baltic St

Kane St

Cheever Pl

Brooklyn Queens Expressway

den Pl

cks St

Tiffany Pl

Willow Pl

Columbia St

Columbia Pl

N

800 metres

Bedford Av

Skillman St

Bedford-Nostrand Avs Ⓜ
G

Franklin Av

Kent Av

Taaffe Pl

Classon Av

Emerson Pl

Steuben St

Grand Av

Ryerson St

Myrtle Av

Hall St

Willoughby Av

Washington Av

Waverly Av

Clinton Av

Vanderbilt Av

Clermont Av

Adelphi St

Carlton Av

Washington Park

Brooklyn Queens Expressway

Flushing Av

Ⓜ Classon Av
G

CLINTON HILL

Monroe St

Madison St

Irving Pl

Quincy St

Lexington Av

Grand Av

Clifton Pl

St James Pl

Dekalb Av

Downing St

Putnam Av

Ⓜ Clinton-Washington Avs Lefferts Pl

Cambridge Pl

8 Locanda Vini + Olii

Clinton-Washington Avs

Ⓜ Clinton-Washington Avs (S stn)
G

Gates Av

Greene Av

2 Brooklyn Flea (S stn)

FORT
GREENE

Cumberland St

S Oxford St

S Portland Av

S Elliot Pl

Fort Greene Pl

St Felix St

Ashland Pl

FORT
GREENE
PARK

Fulton St

Ⓜ Fulton St
G

Lafayette Av

Rockwe

▼ DOWNTOWN BROOKLYN (PAGE 94)

Grand Av

Washington Av

Underhill Av

PROSPECT HEIGHTS

Sterling Pl

St Johns Pl

Lincoln Pl

Eastern Parkway

PROSPECT PARK

Flatbush Av

Prospect Park West

Vanderbilt Av

Butler Pl

Grand Army Plaza

1 Milk Bar

M Grand Army Plaza
2/3

8th Av

Montgomery Pl

Atlantic Av

Pacific St

Dean St

Bergen St

Carlton Av

St Marks Pl

4 James

Prospect Pl

Park Pl

7 Av

M
7th Av

B/Q

PARK SLOPE

M Bergen St
2/3

Flatbush Av

6th Av

6th Av

Prospect Pl

Park Pl

Sterling Pl

St Johns Pl

Lincoln Pl

Berkeley Pl

Union St

President St

7 A Di La

Caroll St

Garfield Pl

1st St

Atlantic Av-Pacific St
B/D/N/Q/R/2/3/4/5

5th Av

M Union St
R

M

Hanson

4th Av

St Marks Pl

3rd Av

300 metres

N

▼ BOERUM HILL & CARROLL GARDENS(PAGE 95)

Coffee & Light Refreshments

Milk Bar

① 620 Vanderbilt Av, at Prospect Place, Prospect Heights
+1 718 230 0844
milkbarbrooklyn.com
Ⓜ 7 Av **Ⓑ Ⓠ**, Grand Army Plaza **②③**
Open daily. Mon-Fri 7.30am-6pm; Sat/Sun 9am-6pm.

A neighbourhood favourite, Milk Bar is suited to occasions as divergent as the passing espresso and the three-hour brunch. Whipping up fantastically strong flat whites, glorious toasts loaded with fluffy eggs, avocado and a plethora of other brunch items, the café marries health and comfort food traditions. The interior blends soft blond wood with exposed brick and vivid primary colour highlights.

Flea Market

Brooklyn Flea

② 176 Lafayette Av, between Clermont Av and Vanderbilt Av, Fort Greene (Sat); East River Waterfront, between North 6th St and North 7th St, Williamsburg (Sun).
brooklynflea.com
Ⓜ Clinton-Washington Avs **Ⓖ**, Clinton-Washington Avs **Ⓒ** (both Fort Greene); Bedford Av **Ⓛ** (Williamsburg)
Open Sat/Sun 10am-5pm; Apr-Nov.

Held on weekends in two distinctive Brooklyn locations, "the Flea" provides a platform for local businesses to showcase a mind-boggling mix of crafted objects, ranging from furniture to textiles to chocolate. Co-founded in 2008 by Jonathan Butler of the Brownstoner blog and Eric Demby, the market has a strong local following, so whether you're after a unique redwood table or a jar of specialized honey, you'll be sure to find it at the flea.

Dumbo Art Space & Shop
Zakka

➌ 155 Plymouth St, between Pearl St
and Jay St, Dumbo
+1 718 801 8037
zakkacorp.com
Ⓜ York St Ⓕ
Open daily noon-7pm.

Located in a brick warehouse in
media savvy Dumbo, Zakka offers
an array of design related gizmos
and gadgets, with a Japanese *je
ne sais quoi*. Whether you're in
the market for the latest book on
drafting or a robotic key chain, look
no further. Once you've made your
purchase, consider taking a walk
through neighbouring Vinegar Hill,
with its picturesque 18th and 19th
century houses originally settled by
Irish immigrants.

Neighbourhood Gem
James

➍ 605 Carlton Av, at St Marks Av,
Prospect Heights
+1 718 942 4255
jamesrestaurantny.com
Ⓜ 7 Av Ⓑ Ⓠ, Bergen St ➋ ➌
Open daily. Mon-Sat 5.30pm-11pm;
Sun 5.30pm-10pm. Brunch Sat/Sun
11am-3.30pm.

James is a visually appealing
neighbourhood restaurant serving
fresh local New American cuisine.
Tucked in a residential corner of
Prospect Heights, the restaurant,
owned by a resident husband and
wife team who pick herbs for the
evening's dishes on a roof next
door, exudes comfortable ease and
calm sophistication. A great spot to
experience contemporary Brooklyn
life.

Bruijkleen Fare

Colonie

⑤ 127 Atlantic Av, between Henry St
and Clinton St, Brooklyn Heights
+1 718 855 7500
colonienyc.com
Ⓜ Court St-Borough Hall Ⓡ ②③④
⑤, Bergen St ⒻⒼ
Open daily. Dinner Mon-Thu 6pm-
10.30pm; Fri 6pm-11.30pm; Sat 5pm-
11.30pm; Sun 5pm-10.30pm. Brunch
Sat/Sun 11am-3pm.

Complete with its own jungle-like
wall foliage and rough-and-tumble
wooden plank ceiling, Colonie
brings high quality farm to table
cuisine and a sophisticated wine list
to a neighbourhood better known
for its brownstone architecture. The
restaurant succeeds on all fronts,
melding architectural aspects of old
Bruijkleen with contemporary NYC's
thriving locavore movement. The
versatile menu ranges from Shrimp
and Grits to Sticky Date Cake.

Kyoto-Style Restaurant

Hibino

⑥ 333 Henry St, at Amity St,
Cobble Hill
+1 718 260 8052
hibino-brooklyn.com
Ⓜ Court St-Borough Hall Ⓡ ②③④
⑤, Bergen St ⒻⒼ
Open daily. Dinner Sun-Thu 5.30pm-
10pm; Fri/Sat 5.30-10.30pm. Lunch
Mon-Fri noon-2.30pm.

Hibino is a unique Kyoto-style
Japanese restaurant nestled among
the quaint old streets of Cobble
Hill. Fresh homemade tofu, *obanzai*
Japanese tapas and authentic
Kyoto-style *oshi* (pressed) sushi
are reason enough to visit, but the
soothing atmosphere makes your
stay particularly enjoyable. Service
is efficient and warm. Though
located just across the river from
the Downtown Manhattan skyline,
this neighbourhood gem feels
worlds away.

Park Slope Trattoria

Al Di La

7 248 5th Av, at Carroll St,
Park Slope
+1 718 783 4565
aldilatrattoria.com
Ⓜ Union St **Ⓡ**
Open daily. Dinner Mon-Thu
6pm-10.30pm; Fri 6pm-11pm; Sat
5.30pm-11pm; Sun 5pm-10pm. Lunch
Mon-Fri noon-3pm. Brunch Sat/Sun
11am-3.30pm.

Exuding warmth and exuberance
in equal doses, this Park Slope
classic has served Venetian dishes
since 1998. The main restaurant's
excellent menu and wine list meld
into the fabulously over the top
chandelier clad rooms. Al Di La Vino,
located around the corner from the
main restaurant, is a more casual
setup serving the same dishes
and stellar wines in a low key, cosy
setting.

Authentic Tuscan

Locanda Vini e Olii

8 129 Gates Av, at Cambridge Place,
Clinton Hill
+1 718 622 9202
locandavinieolii.com
Ⓜ Clinton-Washington Avs **Ⓖ**,
Clinton-Washington Avs **Ⓒ**
Closed Mon. Open Tue-Sun from
5.30pm.

Housed in a beautifully restored
century-old pharmacy, Locanda Vini
e Olii is one of NYC's most authentic
Tuscan restaurants. Genuine
versions of classics running the
gamut from *ribollita* to *pasta e
fagioli* are complemented by an
equally solid Italian wine list. The
restaurant serves as a great culinary
aperitif to a performance at nearby
BAM (p102), which is about a
twenty minute walk (or five minute
cab ride) away, but the superlative
cuisine is a spectacle in of itself.

Pinnacle of the Performing Arts

BAM —Brooklyn Academy of Music

📍 30 Lafayette Av, between Ashland Place and St Felix St, Fort Greene
+1 718 636 4100
bam.org
Ⓜ Atlantic Av-Pacific St Ⓑ Ⓓ Ⓝ Ⓠ
Ⓡ ❷❸❹❺, Fulton St Ⓖ, Lafayette Av Ⓒ
Daily performances. Refer to website for program.

Inaugurated in 1861, when Brooklyn was still an independent city, the Brooklyn Academy of Music has served as a major cultural force ever since. Drawing on deep historical ties with several acclaimed European theatres, BAM hosts top-flight international productions, in addition to maintaining its status as the premier NYC venue for cutting edge new work by local artists. Performances are held at either the intricately restored Harvey Theater (pictured above) or the grandiose Gilman Opera House.

Restaurant & Whiskey Bar

Char No. 4

📍 196 Smith St, between Warren St and Baltic St, Boerum Hill
+1 718 643 2106
charno4.com
Ⓜ Bergen St Ⓕ Ⓖ
Open daily. Dinner Sun-Thu 6pm-midnight; Fri/Sat 6pm-1am. Lunch Fri noon-3.30pm. Brunch Sat/Sun 10am-3.30pm.

Within close proximity of Boerum Hill's most charming brownstone blocks, Char No. 4 serves up rustic *nouveau* American cuisine backed by a stellar list of whiskeys. Flights of Scotch, Irish and American whiskeys are on offer, but the epic list also includes Japanese and other international incarnations. The wild boar sausage is of particular note, as is the top-notch wine list, but it would be hard to leave without giving at least one of the more exotic whiskeys a whirl.

Herbert St
Graham Av
Manhattan Av
Skillman Av
Jackson St
Conselyea St
Metropolitan Av

Brooklyn Queens Expressway

18 Noguchi Museum (Long Island City)

Newton St
Leonard St
Withers St
Frost St
Richardson St
Havemeyer St

Eckford St
Manhattan Av
Lorimer St
Bayard St
Roebling St

GREENPOINT
McCARREN PARK
Union Av
Driggs Av

N 12th St
N 11th St
N 10th St
N 9th St
N 8th St

M Nassau Av
G
Nassau Av
Lorimer St
Guernsey St
Dobbin St
Banker St
N 15th St
N 14th St
N 13th St
Bedford Av

Berry St
17 Hotel Delmano

Wythe Av

Grand St
Powers St
Hooper St
Keap St
Hope St
Rodney St
Borinquen Pl
S 5th St
Café Moto 16
Broadway
Division Av
Marcy Av M
J/M/Z
Marcy Av
Havemeyer St
Metropolitan Av
Hope St
Roebling St
Fillmore Pl
Broadway
Roebling St
S 8th St
S 5th St
Driggs Av
15 Dressler
11 Egg
N 5th St
N 4th St
N 3rd St
N 1st St
Grand St
S 1st St
S 2nd St
S 3rd St
S 4th St
Bedford Av
Williamsburg Bridge
14 Diner S 6th St
13 Brooklyn Oenology
12 Mast Brothers
Berry St
200 metres
Wythe Av

WILLIAMSBURG

N

Williamsburg Brunch

Egg

⑪ 135 North 5th St, between Berry
St and Bedford Av
+1 718 302 5151
pigandegg.com
Ⓜ Bedford Av Ⓛ
Open daily. Mon-Fri 7am-6pm; Sat/
Sun 8am-6pm.

A bright little brunch spot at the
epicentre of the Williamsburg
hipsterhood, Egg serves a full
lunch and dinner menu, but the
breakfasty vibe predominates with
a force. The most important meal
of the day is served with gusto until
6pm on weekends—so roll in at
4pm with a copy of the New York
Times and enjoy a proper breakfast
with the rest of the local night owls.

Chocolate Manufacturer

Mast Brothers

⑫ 105A North 3rd St, between
Wythe Av and Berry St
+1 718 388 2625
mastbrotherschocolate.com
Ⓜ Bedford Av Ⓛ
Closed Mon. Open Tue-Sun noon-
7pm.

A quality-driven local chocolate
house, the Mast Brothers factory,
started by notoriously long bearded
brothers Rick and Michael Mast,
produces an array of delectable
hand crafted chocolates. Single
estate chocolates and subtle blends
are complemented by more exotic
"pairings", such as Vanilla & Smoke,
Stumptown Coffee and Maine
Sea Salt. To accompany the subtle
elegance of the chocolate's flavor,
each bar's intricate wrapping paper,
resembling 19th century wallpaper,
offers a stunning visual feast.

New York State Wines

Brooklyn Oenology

🔞 209 Wythe Av, #106, between North 3rd St and North 4th St
+1 718 599 1259
brooklynoenology.com
Ⓜ Bedford Av Ⓛ
Open daily. Mon 4pm-11pm; Tue/Wed 2pm-10pm; Thu 2pm-11pm; Fri 2pm-midnight; Sat noon-midnight; Sun noon-10pm.

Located among yoga studios and bakeries in a renovated red brick building in the heart of Williamsburg, Brooklyn Oenology marries local wine with local art in a combined wine bar/retail store setting. Patrons can sample a wide array of New York State wines from the North Fork of Long Island and the Finger Lakes, the State's two premier wine producing regions. BOE produces its own range of wines; crushed, fermented and matured at their Long Island facility. Bottles feature labels designed by local artists.

Nouveau Diner

Diner

🔞 85 Broadway, at Berry St
+1 718 486 3077
dinernyc.com
Ⓜ Marcy Av Ⓙ Ⓩ Ⓜ, Bedford Av Ⓛ
Open daily. Dinner 6pm-midnight. Lunch Mon-Fri 11am-5pm. Brunch Sat/Sun 10am-4pm.

Diner is an unusual restaurant offset by the Williamsburg Bridge in a quirky corner of the borough. The food menu is exquisitely executed and the wine list is diverse, nuanced and selective. In line with the general vibe of this *nouveau* diner, the clientele ranges from artist to hipster to foodie. Set slightly apart from the neighbourhood's mainstay, Bedford Avenue, Diner exposes an edgier, intensely appealing aspect of Williamsburg's character.

South Williamsburg Glamour

Dressler

15 149 Broadway, between Bedford
Av and Driggs Av
+1 718 384 6364
dresslernyc.com
M Marcy Av **J Z M**, Bedford Av **L**
Open daily. Mon-Thu 6pm-11pm;
Fri 6pm-midnight; Sat 5.30pm-
midnight; Sun 5.30pm-10.30pm.
Brunch Sun 11am-3.30pm.

From its baroque decor to its
clad-in-black wait staff, a festive
atmosphere predominates at
Michelin-starred Dressler. Playful
and sophisticated, the space is
peppered with intricate pieces
by Brooklyn Navy Yard artisan
sculptors. This sumptuous backdrop
contextualizes the menu, consisting
of an intricate hotchpotch of locally
sourced New American cuisine and
an extensive international wine list.
All in all, a decadently pleasurable
experience.

Eclectic Brasserie

Café Moto

16 394 Broadway, at Division Av and
Hooper St
+1 718 599 6895
cafe-moto.com
M Hewes St **J M**, Broadway **G**
Open daily. Dinner 6pm-midnight.
Lunch/Brunch 11am-4pm. Coffee to-
go 7.30am-11am.

Paris meets Brooklyn at this
shabby-chic bistro nestled under
the elevated J-Z train platform.
Moto cooks up a French inspired
storm and offers a wine list to
match its culinary mettle. A host
of unusual brooklynesque culinary
and oenological treasures are
also to be found, including the
alluringly incongruous "Guinness &
Champagne". The decor is bistro-
meets-speakeasy inspired, and
refreshingly rusty.

Williamsburg Speakeasy

Hotel Delmano

🛈 82 Berry St, at North 9th St
+1 718 387 1945
hoteldelmano.com
Ⓜ Bedford Av Ⓛ
Open daily 6pm-2am.

A proper speakeasy-style bar in prime Williamsburg boasting vintage touches ranging form antique mirrors to charmingly cracked basins in the ornate WC. The spirits, cocktail and wine list is vast and includes an excellent selection of single malt scotches, cocktails and champagnes to revive your senses. Hotel Delmano's comprehensive rawbar includes oysters on the half-shell, chilled lobster, crab legs and long-island fluke ceviche.

Isamu Noguchi Garden Museum

Noguchi Museum

🛈 9-01 33rd Road, at Vernon Boulevard, Long Island City
+1 718 204 7088
noguchi.org
Ⓜ Broadway Ⓝ
Closed Mon/Tue. Open Wed-Fri 10am-5pm; Sat/Sun 11am-6pm. Admission $10.

The Noguchi Museum offers insight into this fascinating artist's life and path breaking work. Born in LA and raised in Japan, Noguchi returned to the US as a teenager, eventually attending evening sculpture workshops in the Lower East Side. He later developed his signature lyrical abstract modernist style while partaking in Constantin Brancusi's Paris workshop. Noguchi's Akari light sculptures, which embody the modernist aesthetic without sacrificing the beauty of line and curve, maintain a coveted status worldwide.

Essentials

Airport Transfer

There are feasible ways of getting into the city by public transport, but the best bet is usually to join the taxi queue or book a car service in advance. Taxis are available at each of New York's three major airports at most times. Commonly used car services include Dial 7 (dial7.com, +1 212 777 7777) and Carmel (carmellimo.com, +1 212 666 6666).

John F. Kennedy Airport (JFK): There is a fixed taxi fare of $45 ($52 from Sep 2012) from (but not to) the airport to any destination in Manhattan. During busy times the Long Island Rail Road (LIRR) commuter rail service is a valuable alternative: take the AirTrain light rail shuttle ($5) to Jamaica station, where trains depart for Midtown's Penn Station, every 10 minutes on weekdays ($6.25 fare, 20 minutes travel time). Another option for those with more time than luggage is the subway. From Jamaica station regular subway services are available to Midtown (E train) and Downtown (J/Z trains); both with about one hour travel time.

Newark Airport (EWR): The airport is located in the State of New Jersey and NYC taxis can therefore only drop passengers off. There is a $15 ($17.50 from Sep 2012) surcharge for rides to the airport. Local taxis are available for rides into New York at a rate of about $60. Both taxis and cars will add a $8 toll. Train services operated by New Jersey Transit ($12.50) connect the airport's main line station, accessible via the free AirTrain light rail shuttle, to Penn Station every 20 minutes, with a travel time of around 30 minutes.

LaGuardia Airport (GUA): The airport is located relatively close to the city and the taxi fare to Midtown is typically around $35. The most reliable link to LaGuardia from Manhattan by public transport is the M60 bus to Harlem and the Upper West Side.

Taxis

NYC taxis are plentiful and relatively inexpensive. During late night and off-peak times, a 15 minute ride will take you from Midtown to SoHo for around $15. All New York taxis accept credit cards without a surcharge for trips of any length. An illuminated sign on the roof indicates that a taxi is available.

During rush hour and other busy times, especially weekdays in Midtown and weekends in Downtown, taxis are frequently stuck in traffic. Taking the Subway or walking can be a quicker way to get around. Taxis are also difficult to flag down between 4pm and 5pm, when rush hour coincides with drivers changing shifts.

Subway

The New York City Subway is one of the most comprehensive transit systems in the world and a safe and convenient way to get around the city. Trains run around the clock, although service frequencies are noticeably lower after 11pm and on weekends.

Subway lines are distinguished by either a letter or a number. In Manhattan, up to four lines of the same colour share the same tracks. On these stretches some lines will operate as express services, skipping stations along the way. Express trains are the fastest way to cover long distances within the city, especially during rush hour. The numbered lines tend to be cleaner and more efficient. See p116 for Subway map.

Tickets are available for single rides ($2.50), or unlimited travel on a weekly ($29) or monthly ($104) basis. There are no fare zones and tickets can be used for rides across the entire network. Tickets can be purchased at station vending machines that accept all major credit cards.

Tipping

Tipping is as much a way of life in New York as it is in the rest of America. In restaurants, tip no less than 15%, and 20% or more to reward good service. A good rule of thumb is to double the sales tax on your bill to arrive at the tip. In taxis, tip 10% to 15% but no less than $1. In general, when in doubt whether tipping is appropriate, tip.

Safety

Manhattan and the proximate parts of Brooklyn tend to feel safer, especially at night, than many other North American and European cities. By applying a reasonable degree of common sense, most unpleasant situations can be avoided.

Index

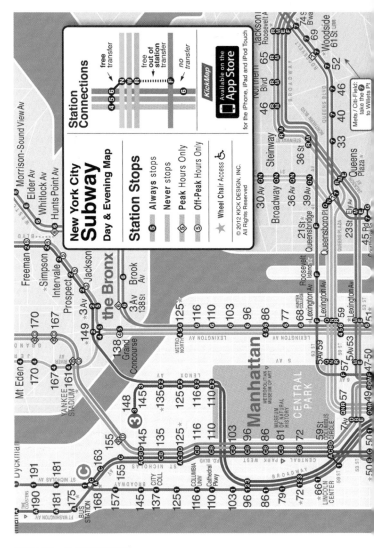

New York City
Subway
Day & Evening Map

Station Stops

- **⑤** Always stops
- **⑤** Never stops
- **⑤** Peak Hours Only
- **⑤** Off-Peak Hours Only
- ★ Wheel Chair Access ♿

Station Connections

free transfer
free out of station transfer
no transfer

KickMap

Available on the
App Store

for the iPhone, iPad and iPod Touch

Mets / Citi-Field:
take the ⑦
to Willets Pt

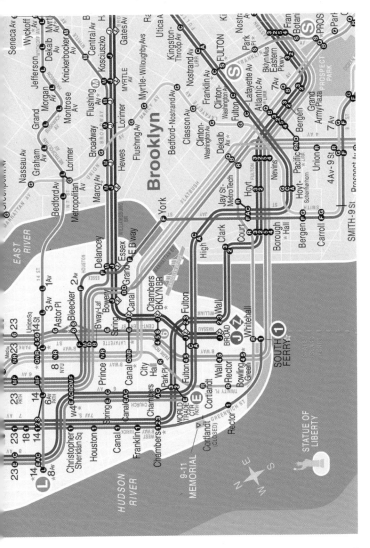

Credits

Published by Analogue Media, LLC
244 5th Avenue, Suite 2446, New York, NY 10001, United States

Edited by Alana Stone
Layout & Production by Stefan Horn

For more information about the Analogue Guides series, or to find out about
availability and purchase information, please visit analogueguides.com

First Edition 2012
ISBN: 978-0-9838585-0-8

Every effort has been made to ensure the accuracy of the information in
this publication. However, some details are subject to change. The publisher
cannot accept responsibility for any loss, injury, inconvenience, or other
consequences arising from the use of this book.

Printed in Spain

Printed on environmentally friendly paper made from 100% recycled
material by mills that are FSC® certified.

Analogue Media would like to thank all contributing venues, designers, manufacturers, agencies and photographers for their kind permission to reproduce their work in this book.

Cover design by Dustin Wallace
Proofread by John Leisure
Kickmap © Kick Design

Photography credits: all images credited to the listed venues unless stated otherwise: (9) Alana Stone (12) left Floto+Warner, right Doug Wolfe (13) left Elizabeth Walker, right Yvonne Brooks (15) both Cynthia Chung (16) left Cynthia Chung, right Michael Harlan Turkell (17) right Francesco Nonnino (18) Cynthia Chung (21) Alana Stone (25) left Paul Brissman (26) left Paul Brissman, right Stefan Horn (27) left Heather Phelps-Lipton (28) left Paul Brissman (29) left Jesse Alexander, right Emily Wolfer (30) right Paul Brissman (31) left Stefan Horn, right Paul Brissman (33) Stefan Horn (36) both Cynthia Chung (37) left Cynthia Chung, right Super Paprika Corp. (38) left Stefan Horn (39) both Cynthia Chung (40) left Cynthia Chung (41) left Cynthia Chung, right Stefan Horn (42) Cynthia Chung (45) Stefan Horn (48) left Stefan Horn, right Larysa Sendich (49) left Peter Aaron/Esto, right Stefan Horn (51) right Stefan Horn (52) left Landmark Theatres, right Stefan Horn (55) Alana Stone (58) left Alex La Cruz (59) left Undine Pöhl, right Alana Stone (60) left Paul Brissman, right Alana Stone (61), left Peter Dressel, right Kirk Bradley Peterkin (62) left Jerry Errico, right Stefan Horn (63) Ari Mintz (65) Stefan Horn (70) right Timothy Hursley (71) both Stefan Horn (72) left Dani Piderman (73) left Stefan Horn, right T Whitney Cox (74) left Ellen Silverman, right Andrew Eccles (75) right Stefan Horn (76) left Stefan Horn, right Sandra Johnson (77) Joshua Bright Photography (79) Alana Stone (84) left David Heald © The Solomon R. Guggenheim Foundation, right Jerry L. Thompson (85) left Michael Bodycomb, right Andre Maier (86) left Stefan Horn (87) Mark Bussell (90) right Adam Reich (91) Paul Brissman (93) Stefan Horn (98) left Paul Brissman, right Kate Glicksberg/Brooklyn Flea (99) left Paul Brissman, right Peter LaMastro (100) left Noah Fecks, right Stefan Horn (101) right Paul Brissman (102) left Ned Witrogen, right Michael Harlan Turkell (106) left Ryan Page, right E. Conor Hagen (107) left Paul Brissman, right Stefan Horn (108) left Stephanie Lempert, right Stefan Horn (109) right Elizabeth Felicella.

About the Series

—A Modern Take on Simple Elegance

Analogue Guides is a series of curated city guidebooks featuring high quality, unique, low key venues—distilled through the lens of the neighbourhood. The guides seek to recapture specificity of place by highlighting aspects of the urban patina frequently lost under the corporate veil of large restaurant groups and ubiquitous chains.

Analogue is local: Analogue Guides delve into the very fabric of the city by taking the neighbourhood as point of reference. Each neighbourhood is complemented by a concise set of sophisticated listings, including restaurants, cafés, bars, hotels and serendipitous finds, all illustrated with photographs. The listings are supplemented by a set of custom designed, user-friendly maps to facilitate navigation of the cityscape.

Analogue is balance: The venues featured in the guides score high on a number of factors, including locally sourced food, tasteful design, a sophisticated and relaxed atmosphere and independent ownership. While we seek excellence across the board, we are not militant with regard to any of these elements but consistently pursue the greatest achievable balance when evaluating listings.

Analogue is convenience: Analogue Guides are designed to complement the internet during pre-travel preparation and smartphones for on-the-ground research. Premium photography and a select choice of venues provide an ideal starting point for pre-travel inspiration. At your destination, the guides serve as portable manuals with detailed neighbourhood maps and clear directions. You will instantly feel at home in the city.